How to for Fireplaces - Hearth, Chimneys, Gas, and Wood-Burning

The Complete Guide to Maintaining, Troubleshooting and Safely Using Your Fireplace

The Fix It Guy

Table of Contents

Introduction

Chapter 1: Fireplace and Chimney Basics
 - Anatomy of a fireplace and chimney
 - How fireplaces and chimneys work
 - Common fireplace and chimney problems to watch out for

Chapter 2: Caring for Your Wood-Burning Fireplace
 - Best practices for using your wood fireplace safely and efficiently
 - Choosing, storing and burning the right firewood
 - Cleaning and maintaining your wood-burning fireplace and chimney
 - Troubleshooting common issues with wood fireplaces

Chapter 3: Mastering Your Gas Fireplace
 - Understanding how gas fireplaces work
 - Safely operating and getting the most out of your gas fireplace
 - Cleaning and upkeep essentials for gas fireplaces
 - Identifying and fixing problems with gas fireplaces

Chapter 4: Maximizing Heat and Efficiency from Your Fireplace
 - Proven techniques to get more heat from wood-burning fireplaces
 - Optimizing heat output and efficiency in gas fireplaces
 - Best tools and accessories for improving fireplace performance

Chapter 5: Hiring Professionals vs DIY Fireplace Care
- When to call in the pros for fireplace and chimney services
    - What to look for when hiring fireplace contractors
    - Fireplace and chimney care tasks you can handle yourself

Chapter 6: Fireplace and Chimney Safety Essentials
    - Fire safety musts for operating fireplaces
    - Chimney and vent safety considerations
    - Childproofing and preventing accidents around fireplaces

Chapter 7: Upgrading, Converting or Adding a Fireplace
    - Options for updating an old fireplace
    - Converting from wood-burning to gas (or vice versa)
    - What to know before adding a new fireplace to your home

Conclusion

Introduction

Picture this: It's a cold, blustery evening, and you're curled up in your favorite armchair, sipping a steaming mug of cocoa. The only sound is the crackling of the fire in your fireplace, casting a warm glow over the room. Feels cozy and inviting, doesn't it?

There's just something magical about fireplaces. Whether it's the mesmerizing dance of the flames, the comforting warmth they provide, or the way they create a central gathering spot for family and friends, fireplaces have an allure that's hard to resist. Not to mention, they can add a touch of elegance and ambiance to any home.

But as much as we love our fireplaces, they can also be a source of frustration and confusion. How do you keep your fireplace burning efficiently and safely? What's the best way to clean your chimney? And what do you do when something goes wrong with your gas fireplace?

That's where this book comes in. "How to Care for Fireplaces" is your ultimate guide to all things fireplace-related. We'll cover everything from the basics of how fireplaces work to advanced troubleshooting techniques for when things go awry.

No matter what type of fireplace you have - wood-burning, gas, or even a wood stove - we've got you covered. We'll walk you through the specific maintenance and care requirements for each type, so you can keep your fireplace in top shape for years to come.

But this book isn't just about the technical aspects of fireplace care. We'll also share some of our favorite tips and tricks for getting the most out of your fireplace. Want to know how to choose the best firewood for a long-lasting, efficient burn? We've got a whole chapter dedicated to that. Curious about how to maximize the heat output from your fireplace? We'll show you some simple hacks that can make a big difference.

By the end of this book, you'll be a bona fide fireplace pro. You'll have the knowledge and confidence to tackle any fireplace-related challenge that comes your way, from routine cleaning to major repairs. And best of all, you'll be able to fully enjoy the warmth, comfort, and beauty that your fireplace provides.

So grab a blanket, settle in by the fire, and let's get started on your journey to becoming a fireplace master. Trust us - your cozy nights at home will never be the same.

Chapter 1
Fireplace and Chimney Basics
Anatomy of a fireplace and chimney

Before we dive into the nitty-gritty of caring for your fireplace, it's essential to understand the basic components and how they work together. In this chapter, we'll take a closer look at the anatomy of a fireplace and chimney, so you can better appreciate the intricacies of these home heating marvels.

Anatomy of a Fireplace and Chimney:

At first glance, fireplaces may seem simple - just a place to burn some logs, right? But there's actually a lot more going on beneath the surface. A properly functioning fireplace and chimney system has several key components that work together to safely and efficiently contain, exhaust, and control the fire and smoke. Let's break it down:

1. Firebox: This is the heart of your fireplace, where the actual fire burns. It's typically made of heat-resistant materials like brick, stone, or metal. The firebox is designed to contain the fire and radiate heat into your living space.

2. Damper: Located above the firebox, the damper is a movable plate that regulates airflow into and out of the chimney. When the damper is open, it allows air to flow up the chimney, fueling the fire and carrying away smoke. When closed, it seals off the chimney to prevent heat loss when the fireplace isn't in use.

3. Smoke chamber: Sitting just above the damper, the smoke chamber is an inverted funnel-shaped space that helps compress and direct smoke and hot gases up into the chimney.

4. Smoke shelf: This is a horizontal surface located behind the damper that helps prevent downdrafts from pushing smoke back into your living space.

5. Flue: The flue is the vertical passageway inside your chimney that carries smoke and exhaust gases up and out of your home. It's typically made of heat-resistant materials like clay tile, stainless steel, or cast iron.

6. Chimney liner: Lining the inside of the flue, the chimney liner helps protect the chimney structure from heat and corrosion, while also improving draft and efficiency. Liners can be made of clay tile, stainless steel, or cast-in-place material.

7. Chimney: The visible portion of your fireplace system, the chimney is the masonry or metal structure that encases and supports the flue. Its primary job is to safely carry smoke and combustion byproducts up and away from your home.

8. Chimney cap: Topping off the chimney, the cap is a fitted metal or masonry cover with mesh sides. It helps keep rain, debris, and critters out of your flue, while allowing smoke to escape.

So how does it all work together? When you light a fire in the firebox, the hot air rises, drawing in fresh air through the open damper. As the smoke and hot gases travel up through the smoke chamber and into the flue, the draft created by the rising heat carries them up and out of the chimney, while also pulling in more fresh air to fuel the fire.

The chimney liner and flue help contain the heat and direct the smoke and gases safely up and out, while the chimney cap keeps the elements and critters from coming down in. And when the damper is closed, it seals off the flue to prevent losing your heated inside air up the chimney when the fireplace isn't in use.

It's a elegantly orchestrated system that, when properly designed and maintained, can provide warmth and comfort for your home for decades. But as you can imagine, with all these hardworking components, there's a lot that can potentially go wrong if your fireplace and chimney aren't properly cared for.

That's why in the coming chapters, we'll take a closer look at maintaining different types of fireplaces and chimneys, troubleshooting common issues, and keeping your system safe and efficient for the long haul. But equipped with this foundational knowledge of how your fireplace works, you're well on your way to becoming a confident and informed fireplace owner. So pat yourself on the back, throw another log on the fire, and let's keep learning!

How fireplaces and chimneys work

Now that we've covered the basic anatomy of a fireplace and chimney, let's take a closer look at how these components work together to create a warm, inviting fire in your home.

At its core, a fireplace and chimney system is designed to safely contain and exhaust the byproducts of combustion - namely, smoke, gases, and heat. But to do this effectively, the system relies on a delicate balance of air pressure, temperature, and flow. Let's explore the science behind how your fireplace and chimney work.

1. The Combustion Process:
When you light a fire in your fireplace, you're initiating a chemical reaction called combustion. As the fuel (wood, gas, etc.) burns, it releases heat, light, smoke, and gases like carbon dioxide and carbon monoxide. For combustion to occur, three key elements are needed: fuel, heat, and oxygen.

2. The Role of Oxygen:
As the fire burns, it consumes oxygen from the surrounding air. This creates a pressure difference between the air inside the firebox and the air outside. As a result, fresh air is drawn into the firebox through the open damper, providing a continuous supply of oxygen to keep the fire burning.

3. The Stack Effect:
As the fire heats the air in the firebox and chimney, that air expands and becomes less dense. This hot, buoyant air naturally wants to rise, creating an updraft in the chimney known as the "stack effect." This updraft is what carries the smoke and gases up and out of your home.

4. The Importance of Draft:

For your fireplace to function properly, it needs a strong, stable draft. Draft is the force that pulls air and combustion byproducts up through the chimney. Several factors can affect draft, including the height and diameter of your chimney, outdoor temperature, and air pressure.

5. The Chimney Effect:

As hot air rises up the chimney, it creates a low-pressure area inside the flue. This pressure difference pulls in more air from the firebox, which in turn fuels the fire and keeps the cycle going. This continuous cycle of rising hot air and inflowing fresh air is what's known as the "chimney effect."

6. Exhaust and Ventilation:

As the hot air and combustion byproducts rise up the flue, they cool and condense on the chimney walls. This is where the chimney liner comes into play - it protects the chimney structure from heat damage and corrosion while also helping to insulate the flue and maintain a strong draft.

7. The Role of the Damper:

The damper plays a crucial role in regulating airflow and controlling the fire. When the damper is open, it allows air to flow freely into the firebox and up the chimney. This airflow is what sustains the fire and carries away smoke and gases. When the damper is closed, it seals off the flue, preventing inside air from escaping up the chimney when the fireplace isn't in use.

So, to recap - when you light a fire, the heat and rising air create a pressure difference that draws in fresh oxygen to fuel the combustion process. As the hot air and gases rise up the flue, they create a continuous cycle of updraft and inflow that keeps the fire burning steadily.

The chimney liner and flue help protect the chimney structure while maintaining a strong draft to carry the exhaust safely up and out of your home.

It's a fascinating interplay of physics and chemistry that's been keeping homes warm for centuries. But as you can imagine, there's a lot that can disrupt this delicate balance - from blockages and buildup in the flue to problems with the damper or chimney cap.

That's why regular maintenance and care are so important for keeping your fireplace and chimney system working safely and efficiently. In the coming chapters, we'll explore some of the most common issues that can arise, and show you how to troubleshoot and prevent them like a pro.

Common fireplace and chimney problems to watch out for

While a well-maintained fireplace and chimney can provide warmth and comfort for years, there are a number of issues that can arise over time. Knowing what to look out for and how to address potential problems is key to enjoying your fireplace safely and efficiently. In this section, we'll cover some of the most common fireplace and chimney issues homeowners face.

1. Creosote Buildup:

One of the most common and potentially dangerous problems is creosote buildup. Creosote is a sticky, flammable substance that forms when wood smoke condenses on the cool walls of the chimney. Over time, this buildup can restrict airflow and even catch fire, leading to a dangerous chimney fire.

To prevent creosote buildup, it's important to burn only dry, seasoned wood, and to have your chimney professionally cleaned and inspected at least once a year. Signs of creosote buildup include difficulty starting or maintaining a fire, smoke filling the room, and a strong, acrid smell.

2. Chimney Blockages:

Another common issue is blockages in the chimney. These can be caused by a variety of factors, including animal nests, fallen leaves and debris, and even structural damage to the chimney itself. A blocked chimney can restrict airflow, leading to smoke and carbon monoxide backing up into your living space.

Regular chimney inspections can help identify and remove blockages before they become a serious problem. Signs of a blocked chimney include smoke filling the room, a strong, unpleasant odor, and visibly damaged or missing chimney components.

13

3. Damper Issues:

The damper is a crucial component of your fireplace system, regulating airflow and helping to control the fire. Over time, dampers can become stuck, warped, or damaged, leading to problems with your fireplace's performance.

A stuck or damaged damper can allow heat and air to escape up the chimney when the fireplace isn't in use, leading to energy inefficiency and higher heating bills. It can also make it difficult to start or maintain a fire, and can even lead to dangerous smoke and gas buildup in your home.

Regular inspection and maintenance of your damper can help prevent these issues. Signs of damper problems include difficulty opening or closing the damper, a noticeable draft even when the damper is closed, and smoke or gas entering the living space.

4. Masonry Damage:

Over time, the masonry structure of your chimney can become damaged due to exposure to the elements, settling of the house, or even chimney fires. Cracks, gaps, and spalling (flaking or chipping) of the bricks and mortar can allow water to seep in, leading to further damage and even structural instability.

Regular inspection of your chimney's masonry and prompt repair of any damage is crucial for maintaining the safety and integrity of your fireplace system. Signs of masonry damage include visible cracks or gaps, flaking or missing bricks, and white staining (efflorescence) on the chimney exterior.

5. Flue Liner Damage:

The flue liner is a critical component of your chimney system, protecting the masonry from heat and corrosion while helping to maintain a strong, stable draft. Over time, flue liners can become cracked, chipped, or even completely deteriorated, leading to serious safety and performance issues.

A damaged flue liner can allow heat and gases to escape into the chimney structure, potentially leading to a house fire. It can also allow creosote and other combustion byproducts to build up more quickly, increasing the risk of a chimney fire.

Regular inspection of your flue liner and prompt repair or replacement of any damage is essential for maintaining a safe and efficient fireplace. Signs of flue liner damage include visible cracks or holes, flaking or missing tiles, and a strong, acrid smell when the fireplace is in use.

By keeping an eye out for these common issues and addressing them promptly with professional help, you can enjoy your fireplace with peace of mind for years to come. In the next chapter, we'll dive into the specifics of caring for wood-burning fireplaces - from choosing the right fuel to cleaning and maintenance tips that will keep your fireplace in top shape.

Chapter 2
Caring for Your Wood-Burning Fireplace
Best practices for using your wood fireplace safely and efficiently

There's nothing quite like the warmth and ambiance of a wood-burning fireplace. The crackle of the logs, the dancing flames, and the cozy heat all combine to create a truly inviting atmosphere in your home. But to enjoy your wood fireplace safely and efficiently, there are some important best practices to follow. In this section, we'll cover the key steps for using and maintaining your wood-burning fireplace like a pro.

Best Practices for Using Your Wood Fireplace Safely and Efficiently:

1. Choose the Right Fuel:
The first step to a safe and efficient fire is choosing the right fuel. Hardwoods like oak, maple, and hickory are the best choices for fireplaces, as they burn slowly and evenly, producing more heat and less smoke than softer woods. Avoid burning green or unseasoned wood, as it contains more moisture and will produce more smoke and creosote buildup.

It's also important to avoid burning treated wood, painted wood, or any kind of trash or debris in your fireplace. These materials can release harmful chemicals and toxins into your home, and can even damage your fireplace and chimney over time.

2. Build a Safe and Efficient Fire:

Once you've chosen your fuel, it's time to build your fire. Start by opening the damper fully to ensure proper airflow. Then, crumple some newspaper and place it in the center of the firebox. Around the newspaper, arrange some kindling in a pyramid shape, with smaller pieces on the bottom and larger pieces on top.

Next, add a few small logs around the kindling, being careful not to overload the firebox. Light the newspaper and allow the kindling and small logs to catch before adding larger logs. As the fire grows, you can add more logs as needed, but be sure to leave space between them for air to circulate.

3. Maintain Proper Airflow:

Proper airflow is key to a safe and efficient fire. Once your fire is burning well, you can adjust the damper to control the flow of air and the size of the flames. A fully open damper will produce a larger, hotter fire, while a partially closed damper will create a slower, more controlled burn.

It's important to avoid closing the damper completely while a fire is burning, as this can cause smoke and gases to back up into your living space. Always wait until the fire has died down completely before closing the damper.

4. Keep Your Fireplace and Chimney Clean:

Regular cleaning and maintenance are crucial for the safety and efficiency of your wood-burning fireplace. Creosote buildup can restrict airflow and even catch fire, leading to a dangerous chimney fire. To prevent this, have your chimney professionally cleaned and inspected at least once a year, or more often if you use your fireplace frequently.

In between professional cleanings, you can help keep your fireplace and chimney cleaner by burning only dry, seasoned wood, and by avoiding overloading the firebox. After each fire, allow the ashes to cool completely before removing them with a metal scoop and disposing of them in a metal container outside your home.

5. Protect Your Home and Family:
Finally, it's important to take steps to protect your home and family when using your wood-burning fireplace. Always use a sturdy fireplace screen to prevent sparks and embers from escaping into your living space. Keep flammable materials like curtains, furniture, and décor at least three feet away from the fireplace opening.

If you have young children or pets, consider using a fireplace gate or barrier to keep them safely away from the flames. And always make sure your smoke and carbon monoxide detectors are in working order, with fresh batteries installed regularly.

By following these best practices for using and maintaining your wood-burning fireplace, you can enjoy all the warmth and ambiance of a crackling fire while keeping your home and family safe. In the next section, we'll take a closer look at choosing, storing, and burning the best firewood for your needs.

Choosing, storing and burning the right firewood

The key to a successful and enjoyable wood-burning fireplace experience lies in the quality of your firewood. Choosing the right wood, storing it properly, and burning it efficiently can make all the difference in the heat output, longevity, and safety of your fires. In this section, we'll cover everything you need to know about selecting, storing, and using the best firewood for your needs.

1. Choosing the Right Firewood:

As mentioned earlier, hardwoods like oak, maple, hickory, and ash are the best choices for firewood. These dense woods burn slowly and evenly, producing more heat and less smoke than softer woods like pine or cedar. Hardwoods also produce longer-lasting coals, which can help keep your fire going for hours.

When selecting firewood, look for pieces that are dry, seasoned, and free of rot or insect infestation. Seasoned wood has been cut, split, and allowed to dry for at least six months to a year, depending on the species and climate. Properly seasoned wood should have a moisture content of 20% or less, which can be measured with a moisture meter.

Avoid using green or unseasoned wood, as it contains more moisture and will produce more smoke, less heat, and more creosote buildup in your chimney. Burning green wood can also be harder to ignite and keep burning, leading to frustration and wasted effort.

2. Storing Firewood Properly:

Once you've selected your firewood, it's important to store it properly to ensure it remains dry and ready to use. The best way to store firewood is in a covered, outdoor area with good air circulation. This could be a dedicated woodshed, a covered porch, or even a simple tarp-covered stack in your yard.

When stacking your firewood, make sure to keep it off the ground to prevent moisture and insect infiltration. You can use a pallet, a few 2x4s, or even some old bricks to create a raised platform for your wood stack. Arrange the wood in a criss-cross pattern, with the ends facing out, to allow for maximum air circulation.

If possible, store your firewood at least 20 feet away from your home to reduce the risk of termite or other insect infestation. And be sure to rotate your stock regularly, using the oldest and driest wood first to ensure a consistent supply of quality firewood.

3. Burning Firewood Efficiently:

Once you have your seasoned firewood stacked and ready to go, it's time to put it to use in your fireplace. To get the most heat and efficiency out of your firewood, follow these tips:

- Start with a small, hot fire using plenty of kindling and a few small logs. This will help establish a good bed of coals and get your firebox up to temperature quickly.
- As the fire grows, add larger logs gradually, placing them on top of the coals and allowing plenty of space for air to circulate. Avoid overloading the firebox, which can smother the flames and produce more smoke.
- Use a fireplace grate to elevate the logs and allow air to flow underneath them. This will help the fire burn more efficiently and produce more heat.

- Adjust the damper as needed to control the airflow and size of the flames. A fully open damper will produce a larger, hotter fire, while a partially closed damper will create a slower, more controlled burn.
- Avoid burning too many logs at once, as this can produce more smoke and creosote buildup. A good rule of thumb is to burn no more than three or four logs at a time, depending on their size and the size of your firebox.

By following these tips for choosing, storing, and burning firewood, you can enjoy all the benefits of a wood-burning fireplace while minimizing the work and maximizing the heat. With a little practice and patience, you'll be a firewood pro in no time!

In the next section, we'll explore some troubleshooting tips and solutions for common issues that can arise with wood-burning fireplaces.

Cleaning and maintaining your wood-burning fireplace and chimney

Regular cleaning and maintenance are essential for the safe and efficient operation of your wood-burning fireplace. Neglecting these tasks can lead to a variety of problems, from decreased heat output and increased smoke to dangerous chimney fires and carbon monoxide leaks. In this section, we'll cover the key steps for keeping your fireplace and chimney in top shape, from routine cleaning to professional inspections.

1. Routine Fireplace Cleaning:
The first step in maintaining your wood-burning fireplace is to clean it regularly. This means removing ashes and debris after each use, as well as periodically cleaning the firebox, grate, and other components. Here's how to do it:

- Allow the ashes to cool completely before attempting to clean the fireplace. This can take up to 24 hours, so plan accordingly.
- Using a metal shovel or scoop, remove the ashes from the firebox and place them in a metal container with a tight-fitting lid. Avoid using a vacuum or plastic container, as these can pose a fire risk.
- Using a stiff-bristled brush, scrub the walls and floor of the firebox to remove any remaining ash, soot, or creosote buildup. Pay extra attention to the corners and crevices where debris can accumulate.
- Clean the fireplace grate and any other metal components with a wire brush to remove any rust or buildup. If necessary, apply a coat of high-temperature paint to prevent further corrosion.
- Sweep or vacuum the area around the fireplace to remove any stray ashes or debris.

2. Chimney Sweeping and Inspection:

In addition to routine fireplace cleaning, it's important to have your chimney professionally swept and inspected at least once a year. This is because creosote, a sticky, flammable substance produced by burning wood, can build up on the walls of your chimney over time. If left unchecked, this buildup can restrict airflow, reduce efficiency, and even catch fire, leading to a dangerous chimney fire.

During a chimney sweeping, a professional will use specialized brushes and tools to remove creosote and other debris from the inside of your chimney. They will also inspect the chimney for any signs of damage, such as cracks, gaps, or missing bricks, and recommend any necessary repairs.

If you use your fireplace frequently or burn a lot of softwood or unseasoned wood, you may need to have your chimney swept more than once a year. A good rule of thumb is to have it swept any time the creosote buildup reaches 1/8 inch thick.

3. Damper Maintenance:

The damper is a critical component of your fireplace system, regulating airflow and helping to control the fire. Over time, the damper can become stuck, warped, or damaged, leading to problems with your fireplace's performance. To keep your damper in good working order, follow these tips:

- Open and close the damper before each use to ensure it is moving freely and not stuck or jammed.
- Inspect the damper for any signs of damage, such as cracks, gaps, or warping. If you notice any issues, have them repaired by a professional.
- Lubricate the damper hinge and handle with a high-temperature lubricant to prevent sticking and ensure smooth operation.

4. Firebox and Masonry Repair:

Over time, the intense heat and exposure to the elements can take a toll on your fireplace's firebox and masonry. Cracks, gaps, and spalling (flaking or chipping) of the bricks and mortar can allow water to seep in, leading to further damage and even structural instability. To prevent these issues, have your fireplace and chimney inspected regularly for any signs of damage, and repair them promptly.

Small cracks and gaps can often be repaired with a high-temperature caulk or sealant, while larger issues may require more extensive masonry work. If you notice any significant damage or instability, it's best to consult with a professional chimney repair specialist to ensure the job is done safely and correctly.

By following these cleaning and maintenance tips, you can keep your wood-burning fireplace and chimney in top shape for years to come. Remember, a little routine upkeep can go a long way in preventing bigger problems down the road, and ensuring that you can enjoy your fireplace safely and efficiently.

In the next section, we'll explore some common troubleshooting issues that can arise with wood-burning fireplaces, and how to address them like a pro.

Troubleshooting common issues with wood fireplaces

Even with regular cleaning and maintenance, issues can still arise with wood-burning fireplaces. Knowing how to troubleshoot and address these problems can save you time, money, and frustration in the long run. In this section, we'll cover some of the most common issues homeowners face with their wood fireplaces, and provide step-by-step guidance on how to resolve them.

1. Difficulty Starting a Fire:
If you're having trouble getting your fire started, there could be several factors at play. Here are some things to check:

- Wet or unseasoned wood: Make sure you're using dry, seasoned firewood with a moisture content of 20% or less. Wet or green wood can be difficult to ignite and will produce more smoke.
- Insufficient kindling: Use plenty of small, dry kindling to help get your fire started. Aim for a mix of sizes, from matchstick-thin to pencil-thick.
- Drafty fireplace: If your fireplace is too drafty, it can be difficult to get a fire going. Make sure the damper is open and the flue is clear, and consider using a fireplace screen to help contain the heat and flames.
- Cold flue: If your chimney is cold, it can take longer for the draft to establish and the fire to catch. Try holding a lit, rolled-up newspaper near the opening of the flue to help warm it up and get the air moving.

2. Excessive Smoke:
If your fireplace is producing a lot of smoke, it can be unpleasant and even dangerous. Here are some common causes and solutions:

- Wet or unseasoned wood: As mentioned above, burning wet or green wood can produce a lot of smoke. Stick to dry, seasoned firewood for best results.
- Closed damper: Make sure the damper is fully open before starting your fire. A closed or partially closed damper can restrict airflow and cause smoke to back up into your living space.
- Dirty chimney: A buildup of creosote or debris in your chimney can restrict airflow and cause smoke to linger. Have your chimney professionally cleaned and inspected to resolve this issue.
- Downdraft: If the air pressure outside is higher than inside your home, it can cause a downdraft that pushes smoke back into your living space. Try opening a window or door near the fireplace to equalize the pressure and allow the smoke to rise up the chimney.

3. Poor Heat Output:

If your fireplace isn't producing enough heat, there could be several reasons why. Here are some things to check:

- Inadequate firewood: Make sure you're using enough firewood to produce a robust fire. Aim for a mix of sizes, from small kindling to larger logs, and replenish the wood as needed to keep the fire burning hot.
- Incorrect burning technique: Building your fire correctly can make a big difference in heat output. Start with a small, hot fire using plenty of kindling, and add larger logs gradually as the fire grows. Avoid overloading the firebox, which can smother the flames and reduce heat output.
- Drafty fireplace: If your fireplace is too drafty, it can allow heat to escape up the chimney instead of radiating into your living space. Consider using a fireplace insert or glass doors to help contain the heat and improve efficiency.

- Dirty or damaged chimney: A buildup of creosote or damage to your chimney can restrict airflow and reduce heat output. Have your chimney professionally cleaned and inspected to resolve these issues.

4. Odd Smells:

If you notice odd smells coming from your fireplace, it could be a sign of a problem. Here are some common causes and solutions:

- Creosote buildup: A strong, acrid smell can indicate a buildup of creosote in your chimney. This is a serious fire hazard and should be addressed by a professional chimney sweep as soon as possible.
- Animal nests: If you smell a strong, musty odor, it could be a sign of an animal nest or debris in your chimney. Have your chimney inspected and cleaned to remove any blockages and prevent further issues.
- Moisture: A damp, musty smell can indicate moisture in your chimney or fireplace. This can be caused by a leak in the chimney or flashing, or by condensation from burning wet or green wood. Address any leaks promptly and make sure to burn only dry, seasoned firewood to prevent moisture buildup.

By troubleshooting these common issues and taking steps to address them, you can keep your wood-burning fireplace running safely and efficiently. Remember, if you're unsure about how to resolve a problem or if you notice any serious issues like cracks, gaps, or structural damage, it's always best to consult with a professional chimney repair specialist.

In the next chapter, we'll shift gears and explore the world of gas fireplaces, including how they work, how to maintain them, and how to troubleshoot common issues.

Chapter 3
Mastering Your Gas Fireplace
Understanding how gas fireplaces work

Gas fireplaces have become increasingly popular in recent years, thanks to their convenience, efficiency, and ease of use. Unlike wood-burning fireplaces, gas fireplaces don't require hauling wood, building a fire, or cleaning up ashes. With the flip of a switch or the push of a button, you can enjoy a cozy, warm fire in seconds. In this chapter, we'll take a closer look at how gas fireplaces work, so you can better understand and appreciate this modern heating marvel.

Understanding How Gas Fireplaces Work:

At their core, gas fireplaces operate on the same basic principles as any other gas appliance, like a stove or furnace. They use either natural gas or propane as fuel, which is ignited by a pilot light or electronic ignition system to create a controlled flame. The heat from this flame is then used to warm the air in your living space, either directly or indirectly, depending on the type of gas fireplace you have.

There are three main types of gas fireplaces: inserts, built-ins, and log sets. Each type works a bit differently, but they all rely on the same basic components to function safely and efficiently. Let's take a closer look at each of these components and how they work together:

1. Gas Supply:
The first component of any gas fireplace is the gas supply. This is typically either natural gas, which is supplied by a local utility company, or propane, which is stored in a tank on your property.

The gas is delivered to your fireplace through a series of pipes and valves, which regulate the flow and pressure of the gas to ensure a consistent, controllable flame.

2. Burner:

The burner is the part of the fireplace where the gas is ignited and the flame is produced. It typically consists of a metal tube or pan with small holes or ports drilled into it, which allow the gas to escape and mix with air before being ignited. The size and shape of the burner can vary depending on the type and size of your fireplace, but they all work on the same basic principle.

3. Ignition System:

To light the burner and create a flame, gas fireplaces use either a standing pilot light or an electronic ignition system. A standing pilot light is a small, constantly burning flame that serves as a source of ignition for the main burner. When the gas is turned on, it flows past the pilot light and is ignited, creating the main flame.

Electronic ignition systems, on the other hand, use a spark or hot surface to ignite the gas when it's turned on. These systems are more energy-efficient than standing pilot lights, as they don't require a constant gas flow to maintain the ignition source.

4. Logs and Embers:

To create a realistic looking fire, gas fireplaces use a combination of ceramic logs and embers. The logs are typically made of a lightweight, heat-resistant ceramic material that's molded and painted to look like real wood. They're stacked on top of the burner in a specific arrangement to create a natural-looking flame pattern.

The embers are small pieces of ceramic or glass that are placed around the base of the logs to simulate the look of glowing coals. Some gas fireplaces also use a bed of sand or vermiculite to create a more realistic ember effect.

5. Venting:

Like any gas appliance, gas fireplaces produce byproducts of combustion that need to be safely vented outside your home. Depending on the type of fireplace you have, this venting can be done in a few different ways.

Direct vent fireplaces use a sealed combustion system, where outside air is drawn in for combustion and the exhaust gases are vented back out through a separate pipe. This type of venting is the most efficient and safest, as it doesn't rely on indoor air for combustion or allow any exhaust gases to enter your living space.

Natural vent (also known as B-vent) fireplaces, on the other hand, use indoor air for combustion and vent the exhaust gases out through a chimney or flue. This type of venting is less efficient than direct venting, as it can allow some heat to escape up the chimney, but it's still a safe and effective option for many homes.

Ventless fireplaces, as the name suggests, don't require any venting at all. Instead, they use a special type of gas and burner system that produces very little exhaust, which is then safely dispersed into your living space. While ventless fireplaces are very efficient and can be installed almost anywhere, they're not allowed in some areas due to air quality concerns.

6. Controls:

Finally, gas fireplaces are equipped with a variety of controls that allow you to adjust the flame height, heat output, and other settings. These controls can be manual, like a simple knob or valve, or electronic, like a remote control or wall-mounted thermostat.

Some gas fireplaces also have additional features like blowers or fans, which help to circulate the warm air throughout your living space, or accent lighting, which can create a more dramatic and inviting ambiance.

By understanding how these basic components work together, you can better appreciate the convenience, efficiency, and beauty of your gas fireplace. In the next section, we'll explore some tips and best practices for safely operating and getting the most out of your gas fireplace.

Safely operating and getting the most out of your gas fireplace

Now that you have a better understanding of how gas fireplaces work, let's dive into some tips and best practices for safely operating and getting the most out of your gas fireplace. While gas fireplaces are generally very safe and easy to use, there are still some important precautions and considerations to keep in mind to ensure optimal performance and longevity.

1. Read the Manual:
Before using your gas fireplace for the first time, it's important to carefully read the owner's manual and any other documentation provided by the manufacturer. This will give you specific information on how to safely operate and maintain your particular model of fireplace, as well as any warnings or precautions to be aware of.

2. Have Your Fireplace Professionally Installed and Inspected:
If you're installing a new gas fireplace or converting an existing wood-burning fireplace to gas, it's crucial to have the work done by a qualified professional. Gas fireplaces require specialized knowledge and tools to install safely and correctly, and even a small mistake can lead to dangerous gas leaks or other hazards.

Additionally, it's a good idea to have your gas fireplace professionally inspected and serviced at least once a year, even if you don't notice any problems. A professional technician can check for gas leaks, ensure proper venting and combustion, and make any necessary repairs or adjustments to keep your fireplace running safely and efficiently.

3. Keep the Area Around Your Fireplace Clear:
Just like with a wood-burning fireplace, it's important to keep the area around your gas fireplace clear of any flammable materials like curtains, furniture, or decor. Even though gas fireplaces don't produce sparks or embers like wood fires, the heat from the flames can still ignite nearby objects if they're too close.

As a general rule, keep anything flammable at least three feet away from your gas fireplace, and never place anything directly on or in front of the glass or screen.

4. Don't Use Your Fireplace for Cooking or Heating:
While it may be tempting to roast marshmallows or warm up food over your gas fireplace, it's important to remember that it's not designed for cooking or heating. The ceramic logs and embers in your fireplace are not meant to come into contact with food, and doing so can cause damage or create unsafe conditions.

Similarly, while gas fireplaces can provide a good amount of supplemental heat, they should not be used as your primary heating source. Gas fireplaces are not as efficient or powerful as dedicated heating systems like furnaces or boilers, and relying on them too heavily can lead to higher energy bills and reduced comfort.

5. Know How to Adjust the Flame and Heat Output:
One of the great things about gas fireplaces is that you can easily adjust the flame height and heat output to suit your preferences and needs. Most gas fireplaces have a control knob or remote that allows you to turn the flame up or down, as well as adjust the blower or fan speed if your fireplace has one.

When you first start your fireplace, it's a good idea to keep the flame on the lower side until the fireplace warms up and stabilizes. This can help prevent any sudden "pops" or "bangs" that can occur when cold gas is ignited.

Once your fireplace is warmed up, you can adjust the flame height and blower speed to your liking. Keep in mind that higher flames and blower speeds will produce more heat, but will also use more gas and may be louder.

6. Clean and Maintain Your Fireplace Regularly:

To keep your gas fireplace looking and working its best, it's important to clean and maintain it regularly. This includes wiping down the glass or screen with a soft, damp cloth to remove any dust or debris, as well as vacuuming or brushing out the interior of the fireplace to keep it free of cobwebs, dust, and other buildup.

If you notice any soot or discoloration on the ceramic logs or embers, this is a sign that your fireplace may not be burning as cleanly or efficiently as it should. This can be caused by a variety of factors, including improper venting, dirty burners, or incorrect gas pressure. If you notice persistent soot or discoloration, it's best to have your fireplace inspected by a professional to diagnose and fix the problem.

7. Use a Carbon Monoxide Detector:

Finally, while gas fireplaces are designed to burn very cleanly and produce minimal emissions, it's still a good idea to use a carbon monoxide detector in your home, especially if you have a ventless or natural vent fireplace. Carbon monoxide is an odorless, colorless gas that can be deadly in high concentrations, and even a small gas leak or improper venting can allow it to build up in your home.

By placing a carbon monoxide detector near your gas fireplace and in other key areas of your home, you can be alerted to any potential problems and take action to keep yourself and your family safe.

By following these tips and best practices, you can enjoy all the warmth, comfort, and ambiance of your gas fireplace while also ensuring optimal safety, efficiency, and longevity. Whether you use your fireplace for occasional accent lighting or as a regular source of supplemental heat, a well-maintained and properly operated gas fireplace can be a valuable and enjoyable addition to any home.

Cleaning and upkeep essentials for gas fireplaces

While gas fireplaces are generally much easier to maintain than wood-burning fireplaces, they still require some regular cleaning and upkeep to ensure optimal performance, safety, and longevity. In this section, we'll explore the key cleaning and maintenance tasks that every gas fireplace owner should know and perform on a regular basis.

1. Cleaning the Glass or Screen:

One of the most frequent and noticeable cleaning tasks for gas fireplaces is keeping the glass or screen clear and free of dirt, dust, and soot. Over time, the glass or screen can become hazy or discolored, which can obstruct your view of the flames and reduce the overall ambiance of your fireplace.

To clean the glass or screen, start by turning off your fireplace and allowing it to cool completely. Then, using a soft, damp cloth or sponge, gently wipe down the surface of the glass or screen, taking care not to apply too much pressure or use any abrasive cleaners that could scratch or damage the surface.

For tougher stains or buildup, you can use a mixture of equal parts vinegar and water, or a specialized fireplace glass cleaner. Apply the solution to your cloth or sponge, and gently scrub the affected areas until they're clean. Then, wipe the surface down with a clean, damp cloth to remove any remaining cleaner or residue.

2. Vacuuming and Dusting the Interior:

In addition to cleaning the glass or screen, it's also important to regularly vacuum and dust the interior of your gas fireplace to keep it free of debris, cobwebs, and other buildup. This not only helps to keep your fireplace looking its best, but it can also help to prevent any potential clogs or obstructions in the burners or venting system.

To vacuum and dust your fireplace, start by turning it off and allowing it to cool completely. Then, using a soft brush attachment on your vacuum cleaner, gently go over all the surfaces of the interior, including the ceramic logs, embers, and walls of the firebox. Pay extra attention to any crevices or hard-to-reach areas where dust and debris can accumulate.

If you notice any stubborn dirt or grime that won't come off with vacuuming, you can use a soft, dry brush or cloth to gently scrub the affected areas. Avoid using any water or cleaning solutions inside your fireplace, as this can damage the components or create hazardous conditions when the fireplace is turned back on.

3. Inspecting and Cleaning the Burners:
The burners are the heart of your gas fireplace, and keeping them clean and in good working condition is essential for safe and efficient operation. Over time, the burners can become clogged with dirt, debris, or even insects, which can impede the flow of gas and cause uneven or inconsistent flames.

To inspect and clean your burners, start by turning off the gas supply to your fireplace and allowing it to cool completely. Then, carefully remove the ceramic logs and embers to access the burners underneath. Using a soft brush or cloth, gently clean the surface of the burners, paying extra attention to the ports or holes where the gas comes out.

If you notice any significant buildup or obstructions in the burner ports, you can use a small wire or pipe cleaner to gently clear them out. Be very careful not to damage or enlarge the ports, as this can affect the performance and safety of your fireplace.

Once you've cleaned the burners, carefully replace the logs and embers, making sure they're positioned correctly and securely. Then, turn the gas supply back on and test your fireplace to ensure it's working properly and the flames are even and consistent.

4. Checking and Replacing Batteries:

If your gas fireplace has a remote control, thermostat, or other electronic components, it's important to regularly check and replace the batteries to ensure proper operation. Most gas fireplace remotes and thermostats use standard AA or AAA batteries, which should be replaced at least once a year, or whenever you notice any inconsistencies or delays in the fireplace's response.

To replace the batteries, start by locating the battery compartment, which is usually located on the back or bottom of the remote or thermostat. Carefully remove the old batteries and dispose of them properly, then insert new batteries, making sure they're oriented correctly according to the markings in the compartment.

After replacing the batteries, test your fireplace to ensure it's responding properly to the remote or thermostat commands. If you notice any continuing issues or inconsistencies, it may be a sign of a more serious problem that requires professional attention.

5. Scheduling Professional Maintenance:

While the above cleaning and upkeep tasks can be performed by most homeowners, it's also important to schedule regular professional maintenance for your gas fireplace to ensure optimal safety, efficiency, and longevity. A qualified technician can perform a thorough inspection and cleaning of your entire fireplace system, including the venting, gas lines, and internal components, to identify and address any potential issues before they become serious problems.

Most manufacturers recommend having your gas fireplace professionally serviced at least once a year, preferably before the start of the heating season. During a typical maintenance visit, a technician will:

- Inspect and clean the burners, pilot light, and thermocouple
- Check the gas pressure and adjust it if necessary
- Test the safety shut-off and other safety features
- Inspect the venting system for any leaks, obstructions, or damage
- Clean and calibrate the blower or fan (if applicable)
- Diagnose and repair any other issues or inconsistencies

By scheduling regular professional maintenance, you can have peace of mind knowing that your gas fireplace is operating safely and efficiently, and catch any potential problems early before they turn into costly repairs or safety hazards.

In conclusion, while gas fireplaces are relatively low maintenance compared to wood-burning fireplaces, they still require some regular cleaning and upkeep to ensure optimal performance and longevity. By following the tips and best practices outlined in this section, you can keep your gas fireplace looking and working its best for years to come, and enjoy all the warmth, comfort, and ambiance it has to offer.

Identifying and fixing problems with gas fireplaces

Despite regular cleaning and maintenance, gas fireplaces can still experience various issues that affect their performance, efficiency, and safety. Being able to identify and troubleshoot these problems is an essential skill for any gas fireplace owner, as it can help you determine when a problem requires professional attention and potentially save you time and money on repairs. In this section, we'll explore some of the most common problems that can occur with gas fireplaces and provide step-by-step guidance on how to diagnose and fix them.

1. Pilot Light Issues:

One of the most common problems with gas fireplaces is a pilot light that won't stay lit or won't light at all. The pilot light is a small, constant flame that ignites the main burner when the fireplace is turned on, and if it goes out or becomes obstructed, the fireplace won't function properly.

If your pilot light won't stay lit, the first thing to check is the thermocouple, which is a small metal rod that sits in the pilot flame and generates an electrical current to keep the gas valve open. If the thermocouple is dirty, bent, or damaged, it may not generate enough current to keep the pilot light on.

To clean the thermocouple, start by turning off the gas supply to your fireplace and allowing it to cool completely. Then, using a soft cloth or brush, gently clean the tip of the thermocouple, removing any dirt, debris, or soot. If the thermocouple is bent or damaged, it may need to be replaced by a professional.

Another common cause of pilot light issues is a clogged or dirty pilot orifice, which is the small hole where the gas comes out to feed the pilot flame. If the orifice becomes clogged with dirt or debris, it can prevent the pilot light from getting enough gas to stay lit.

To clean the pilot orifice, start by turning off the gas supply and allowing the fireplace to cool. Then, using a small wire or needle, gently clean out the orifice, taking care not to damage or enlarge it. If the orifice is severely clogged or damaged, it may need to be replaced by a professional.

2. Burner Issues:

Another common problem with gas fireplaces is burners that won't light, won't stay lit, or produce uneven or inconsistent flames. Like pilot light issues, burner problems can often be traced back to dirty or clogged components that restrict the flow of gas.

If your burners won't light or stay lit, the first thing to check is the gas supply. Make sure the gas valve is turned on and there are no leaks or obstructions in the gas line. If the gas supply is functioning properly, the next step is to inspect and clean the burner ports, which are the small holes where the gas comes out to feed the flames.

Using a soft brush or cloth, gently clean the surface of the burners, paying extra attention to the ports. If you notice any significant buildup or obstructions, you can use a small wire or pipe cleaner to carefully clear them out. Be very careful not to damage or enlarge the ports, as this can affect the performance and safety of your fireplace.

If your burners are producing uneven or inconsistent flames, it may be a sign of improper gas pressure or a misaligned or damaged burner. These issues typically require professional diagnosis and repair to ensure safe and efficient operation.

3. Thermostat and Remote Control Issues:
If your gas fireplace has a thermostat or remote control, you may experience issues with the fireplace not responding properly to commands or failing to turn on or off when expected. These problems can often be traced back to dead or weak batteries, loose or faulty wiring connections, or a malfunctioning thermostat or receiver.

If your fireplace is not responding to the thermostat or remote, the first thing to check is the batteries. Replace the batteries in the thermostat or remote with fresh, high-quality batteries and see if that resolves the issue. If the problem persists, check the wiring connections between the thermostat or receiver and the gas valve, making sure they're tight and secure.

If the wiring appears to be in good condition, the issue may be with the thermostat or receiver itself. These components can wear out over time or become damaged by heat, moisture, or other factors. In most cases, a malfunctioning thermostat or receiver will need to be replaced by a professional to restore proper operation.

4. Venting Problems:
Proper venting is essential for the safe and efficient operation of a gas fireplace, as it allows combustion byproducts to be safely expelled outside while drawing in fresh air for the flames. If the venting system becomes damaged, obstructed, or disconnected, it can lead to a variety of problems, including poor flame quality, excessive soot or odors, and even dangerous carbon monoxide buildup.

Some common signs of venting problems include:

- Flames that are excessively blue, lazy, or lift off the burner
- Soot or discoloration on the logs, walls, or glass of the fireplace
- Strong, persistent odors of gas or combustion byproducts
- Hissing, whistling, or roaring sounds coming from the fireplace or vent

If you notice any of these signs, it's important to have your venting system inspected and repaired by a qualified professional as soon as possible. Attempting to diagnose or repair venting problems yourself can be extremely dangerous and may void your fireplace warranty or violate local building codes.

5. Blower or Fan Issues:

If your gas fireplace has a built-in blower or fan to help circulate heat, you may experience issues with the blower not turning on, turning off, or operating at the correct speed. These problems can often be traced back to a faulty or damaged blower motor, loose or disconnected wiring, or a malfunctioning thermostat or speed control.

If your blower isn't turning on or off when it should, the first thing to check is the wiring connections. Make sure the blower is plugged in securely and the connections between the blower and the speed control or thermostat are tight and free of damage. If the wiring appears to be in good condition, the issue may be with the blower motor itself, which can wear out over time or become damaged by heat or debris.

If your blower is operating at the wrong speed or making unusual noises, it may be a sign of a malfunctioning speed control or thermostat. These components can fail due to age, heat, or electrical issues, and may need to be replaced by a professional to restore proper operation.

In conclusion, while gas fireplaces are generally reliable and low-maintenance, they can still experience a variety of problems that affect their performance and safety. By being aware of these common issues and knowing how to diagnose and troubleshoot them, you can help keep your gas fireplace running smoothly and avoid costly repairs or safety hazards. However, if you're ever unsure about how to address a problem or if you notice any signs of gas leaks, venting issues, or other serious concerns, it's always best to err on the side of caution and contact a qualified professional for assistance.

Chapter 4
Maximizing Heat and Efficiency from Your Fireplace
Proven techniques to get more heat from wood-burning fireplaces

While fireplaces are often seen as a cozy and attractive feature in a home, they can also be a valuable source of heat and energy efficiency. However, many homeowners don't realize that there are several techniques and strategies they can use to get the most heat and efficiency out of their fireplaces, especially wood-burning models. In this section, we'll explore some proven techniques for maximizing the heat output and efficiency of your wood-burning fireplace, so you can stay warm and comfortable all winter long while also saving money on your energy bills.

Proven Techniques to Get More Heat from Wood-Burning Fireplaces:

1. Use Seasoned, Dry Firewood:
One of the most important factors in getting more heat from your wood-burning fireplace is using properly seasoned, dry firewood. Freshly cut or "green" wood contains a lot of moisture, which takes a significant amount of energy to burn off before the wood can start producing useful heat. This not only reduces the overall heat output of your fireplace but also produces more smoke and creosote buildup in your chimney, which can be a fire hazard.

To ensure your firewood is properly seasoned, it should be cut, split, and stacked in a dry, covered area for at least six months to a year before burning. Properly seasoned firewood should have a moisture content of 20% or less, which you can check with a moisture meter or by looking for signs like cracks in the end grain and a hollow sound when two pieces are knocked together.

When building a fire, start with smaller, dry kindling to get the flames going, then add larger pieces of seasoned wood as the fire grows. Avoid overloading the fireplace, as this can restrict airflow and reduce heat output. Instead, add a few pieces at a time, allowing each to catch fully before adding more.

2. Install a Fireback:

A fireback is a heavy metal plate that sits at the back of your fireplace, reflecting heat back into the room and helping to increase the overall heat output of your fire. Firebacks are typically made of cast iron or stainless steel and come in a variety of sizes and designs to fit different fireplace openings.

In addition to reflecting heat, firebacks also help to protect the back wall of your fireplace from damage caused by high temperatures and frequent use. They can also add a decorative touch to your fireplace, with many models featuring intricate designs or patterns.

To install a fireback, simply place it against the back wall of your fireplace, making sure it's centered and level. Some models may require brackets or other hardware to secure them in place, while others are freestanding and can be easily removed for cleaning or storage.

3. Use a Fireplace Grate:

A fireplace grate is a metal frame that sits inside your fireplace and holds the firewood off the floor of the firebox. This allows air to circulate around the logs more easily, promoting more complete combustion and increasing heat output.

Fireplace grates come in a variety of sizes and styles to fit different fireplace openings, and can be made of cast iron, steel, or other heat-resistant materials. Some models also feature built-in ash pans or other features to make cleaning and maintenance easier.

When using a fireplace grate, make sure to choose one that's appropriately sized for your fireplace opening and the amount of wood you typically burn. The grate should be sturdy and level, with enough space between the bars to allow ash to fall through without letting logs roll out.

4. Install Glass Doors:

While many homeowners enjoy the open, crackling flames of a traditional wood-burning fireplace, installing glass doors can actually help to increase the heat output and efficiency of your fireplace. Glass doors create a barrier between the room and the fireplace, helping to prevent warm air from escaping up the chimney when the fire isn't burning.

Glass doors also help to reduce drafts and increase the overall temperature of the fire, as the glass reflects heat back into the firebox. This can lead to more complete combustion and less smoke and creosote buildup in your chimney.

When choosing glass doors for your fireplace, look for models that are designed to fit your specific fireplace opening and that feature heat-resistant glass and sturdy, adjustable frames. Some models also include built-in vents or other features to help regulate airflow and temperature.

5. Consider a Fireplace Insert:

If you're looking for a more significant boost in heat output and efficiency, consider installing a fireplace insert. A fireplace insert is essentially a self-contained wood-burning stove that fits inside your existing fireplace opening, providing a more efficient and controllable way to heat your home.

Fireplace inserts are designed to maximize heat output and minimize heat loss, with features like airtight doors, advanced combustion systems, and built-in blowers to circulate warm air throughout your living space. Many models also include thermostatic controls and other features to help you regulate temperature and burn time more easily.

When choosing a fireplace insert, look for models that are appropriately sized for your fireplace opening and that meet or exceed EPA emissions standards for clean, efficient burning. You'll also want to consider factors like heat output, burn time, and ease of use when making your decision.

6. Maintain Your Chimney:
Finally, one of the most important things you can do to maximize the heat output and efficiency of your wood-burning fireplace is to maintain your chimney properly. A dirty or obstructed chimney can restrict airflow, reduce heat output, and increase the risk of chimney fires and other hazards.

To keep your chimney in top condition, have it professionally inspected and cleaned at least once a year, or more often if you use your fireplace frequently. A qualified chimney sweep can remove soot, creosote, and other buildup from the flue and check for any signs of damage or deterioration that could affect performance or safety.

In between professional cleanings, you can also take steps to minimize buildup and maintain good airflow in your chimney. This includes using dry, seasoned firewood, building smaller, hotter fires rather than large, smoldering ones, and avoiding burning any trash, debris, or treated wood in your fireplace.

By following these proven techniques for maximizing heat output and efficiency, you can get the most out of your wood-burning fireplace and enjoy cozy, comfortable warmth all winter long. Whether you're looking to save money on your energy bills, reduce your environmental impact, or simply create a more inviting atmosphere in your home, these strategies can help you achieve your goals and make the most of this timeless and beloved home feature.

Optimizing heat output and efficiency in gas fireplaces

While gas fireplaces are inherently more efficient and convenient than wood-burning models, there are still several strategies and techniques you can use to optimize their heat output and overall efficiency. By making a few simple adjustments and upgrades, you can enjoy even more warmth and comfort from your gas fireplace while also saving money on your energy bills and reducing your environmental impact. In this section, we'll explore some of the most effective ways to optimize the heat output and efficiency of your gas fireplace.

1. Choose the Right Size Fireplace:
One of the most important factors in optimizing the heat output and efficiency of a gas fireplace is choosing the right size unit for your space. A fireplace that's too small may not provide enough heat to warm your room effectively, while one that's too large may waste energy and create uncomfortable hot spots.

To determine the appropriate size gas fireplace for your space, consider factors like the square footage of the room, the height of the ceilings, and the level of insulation in your walls and windows. As a general rule of thumb, you'll want to choose a fireplace with a heat output of around 5,000 to 6,000 BTUs per 100 square feet of room space, depending on your specific climate and heating needs.

It's also important to consider the placement of your gas fireplace within the room. For optimal heat distribution, try to locate the fireplace on an interior wall rather than an exterior one, and avoid placing it too close to windows, doors, or other drafty areas.

2. Install a Blower:

One of the most effective ways to boost the heat output and distribution of a gas fireplace is to install a blower. A blower is essentially a small fan that's mounted inside the fireplace and helps to circulate warm air throughout the room more efficiently.

Most gas fireplace manufacturers offer blower kits that are specifically designed for their units, and can be easily installed by a qualified technician. These kits typically include a variable-speed motor, a heat-activated switch, and a series of ductwork and vents to direct the airflow.

When shopping for a blower kit, look for models that are appropriately sized for your fireplace and that feature high-quality, durable components. You'll also want to consider factors like noise level, energy efficiency, and ease of maintenance when making your selection.

3. Use Ceramic Logs:

While many gas fireplaces come with standard metal or ceramic-fiber logs, upgrading to high-quality ceramic logs can actually help to increase heat output and efficiency. Ceramic logs are designed to mimic the look and feel of real wood, with intricate details and natural coloration that create a more realistic flame pattern.

In addition to their aesthetic benefits, ceramic logs also have excellent heat retention properties, meaning they can absorb and radiate heat more effectively than other materials. This can help to increase the overall temperature of the fireplace and distribute warmth more evenly throughout the room.

When choosing ceramic logs for your gas fireplace, look for models that are appropriately sized for your unit and that feature high-quality, durable construction. Some manufacturers also offer specialized log sets that are designed to enhance specific flame patterns or heat output levels.

4. Adjust the Air Shutter:
Another simple but effective way to optimize the heat output and efficiency of a gas fireplace is to adjust the air shutter. The air shutter is a small, adjustable vent located near the base of the burner that controls the amount of air that mixes with the gas before it ignites.

If the air shutter is set too low, the fireplace may produce a tall, yellow flame that flickers and produces soot and other byproducts. This can reduce heat output and efficiency, and may even pose a safety hazard over time.

On the other hand, if the air shutter is set too high, the fireplace may produce a short, blue flame that doesn't generate much heat and may even blow itself out.

To optimize the air shutter setting on your gas fireplace, start by consulting the manufacturer's instructions or a qualified technician. In general, you'll want to adjust the shutter until the flames are mostly blue with just a hint of yellow at the tips, and are steady and well-defined.

5. Schedule Regular Maintenance:
Finally, one of the most important things you can do to optimize the heat output and efficiency of your gas fireplace is to schedule regular maintenance with a qualified technician. Just like any other gas appliance, a gas fireplace requires periodic cleaning, inspection, and adjustment to ensure safe and efficient operation.

During a typical maintenance visit, a technician will clean and inspect the burner, pilot light, and other key components, check for any signs of wear or damage, and make any necessary adjustments or repairs. They may also clean and calibrate the thermostat, blower, and other accessories to ensure optimal performance.

Depending on the frequency and intensity of use, most gas fireplaces should be professionally serviced at least once a year, either before or after the primary heating season. However, if you notice any signs of poor performance, unusual odors, or other concerns, it's always best to schedule a maintenance visit as soon as possible to diagnose and address any potential issues.

By following these strategies for optimizing heat output and efficiency, you can enjoy even more warmth, comfort, and convenience from your gas fireplace. Whether you're looking to reduce your energy bills, improve your home's overall comfort and ambiance, or simply make the most of this popular and versatile heating option, these techniques can help you achieve your goals and enjoy your fireplace to the fullest.

Best tools and accessories for improving fireplace performance

In addition to the strategies and techniques described in the previous sections, there are also several tools and accessories available that can help to improve the performance, efficiency, and convenience of your fireplace. Whether you have a wood-burning or gas model, these items can help you get the most out of your fireplace and enjoy a more comfortable, hassle-free heating experience. In this section, we'll explore some of the best tools and accessories for improving fireplace performance.

1. Fireplace Grate:

As mentioned earlier, a fireplace grate is a metal frame that sits inside the firebox and holds the logs off the floor, allowing for better airflow and more efficient combustion. For wood-burning fireplaces, a high-quality grate is essential for achieving optimal heat output and reducing smoke and other byproducts.

When shopping for a fireplace grate, look for models that are made from durable, heat-resistant materials like cast iron or stainless steel, and that feature a sturdy, well-balanced design. Some grates also come with built-in ash pans or other features that can make cleaning and maintenance easier.

2. Fireplace Screen:

A fireplace screen is a mesh or glass barrier that sits in front of the firebox and helps to prevent sparks, embers, and other debris from escaping into the room. For wood-burning fireplaces, a screen is an essential safety feature that can help to protect your floors, furniture, and loved ones from accidental burns or fire hazards.

When choosing a fireplace screen, look for models that are appropriately sized for your firebox opening and that feature a sturdy, durable frame and tight-fitting mesh or glass panels. Some screens also come with decorative accents or finishes that can enhance the overall look of your fireplace.

3. Fireplace Tools:

Another essential accessory for any fireplace is a set of high-quality tools for tending the fire and keeping the firebox clean. A basic tool set typically includes a poker for adjusting logs and coals, a brush and shovel for removing ash and debris, and a pair of tongs for gripping and moving logs safely.

When shopping for fireplace tools, look for models that are made from durable, heat-resistant materials like wrought iron or stainless steel, and that feature comfortable, ergonomic handles for easy gripping. Some tool sets also come with additional accessories like a log rack or bellows for stoking the fire.

4. Chimney Cap:

A chimney cap is a small, cage-like device that sits at the top of your chimney and helps to keep out rain, snow, debris, and animals while allowing smoke and other byproducts to escape safely. For both wood-burning and gas fireplaces, a chimney cap is an essential accessory that can help to prevent damage, blockages, and other issues that can affect performance and safety.

When choosing a chimney cap, look for models that are appropriately sized for your flue opening and that feature a sturdy, weather-resistant construction and tight-fitting mesh or wire screens. Some caps also come with additional features like spark arrestors or built-in dampers for added safety and convenience.

5. Fireplace Insert:

For homeowners looking to upgrade the performance and efficiency of an existing wood-burning fireplace, a fireplace insert can be an excellent investment. As described earlier, an insert is essentially a self-contained wood-burning stove that fits inside the existing firebox and uses advanced combustion technology and heat exchange systems to maximize heat output and minimize emissions.

When shopping for a fireplace insert, look for models that are appropriately sized for your firebox opening and that meet or exceed EPA certification standards for clean, efficient burning. You'll also want to consider factors like heat output, burn time, and ease of use when making your selection, as well as any additional features like built-in blowers or thermostatic controls.

6. Gas Logs:

For homeowners with gas fireplaces, one of the simplest and most effective ways to improve performance and ambiance is to upgrade to high-quality gas logs. As mentioned earlier, gas logs are designed to mimic the look and feel of real wood, with intricate details and natural coloration that create a more realistic flame pattern.

When choosing gas logs for your fireplace, look for models that are appropriately sized for your firebox and that feature high-quality, heat-resistant materials like ceramic or refractory cement. Some manufacturers also offer specialized log sets with built-in burners or other features that can enhance heat output and efficiency.

7. Thermostat:

Finally, for homeowners with gas fireplaces, a programmable thermostat can be an excellent tool for optimizing comfort and efficiency. By allowing you to set specific temperature ranges and schedules for your fireplace, a thermostat can help you maintain a consistent, comfortable environment while also reducing energy waste and costs.

When shopping for a fireplace thermostat, look for models that are compatible with your specific fireplace and that offer easy, intuitive controls and programming options. Some thermostats also come with additional features like remote access, voice control, or smart home integration for added convenience and flexibility.

By investing in these tools and accessories, you can take your fireplace performance and enjoyment to the next level. Whether you're looking to enhance safety, efficiency, convenience, or ambiance, these items can help you get the most out of your fireplace and create a warm, inviting atmosphere in your home. So why wait? Start exploring your options today and discover how these simple upgrades can transform your fireplace experience!

Chapter 5
Hiring Professionals vs DIY Fireplace Care

When to call in the pros for fireplace and chimney services

When it comes to maintaining and repairing your fireplace and chimney, it's important to know when to tackle projects yourself and when to call in the professionals. While some basic tasks like cleaning and minor maintenance can often be handled by homeowners with the right tools and knowledge, other more complex or high-stakes jobs are best left to trained and certified experts. In this section, we'll explore some key considerations for deciding between hiring professionals and DIY fireplace care, with a particular focus on when to call in the pros for fireplace and chimney services.

When to Call in the Pros for Fireplace and Chimney Services:

1. Annual Inspections:
One of the most important times to call in a professional is for your annual fireplace and chimney inspection. Even if you don't notice any obvious problems or performance issues, having your system thoroughly inspected by a trained technician at least once a year is essential for identifying and addressing any potential safety hazards or maintenance needs.

During an annual inspection, a professional will typically check for things like:

- Creosote buildup and other blockages in the flue
- Cracks, gaps, or other damage to the chimney structure or lining

- Proper clearance and ventilation for the fireplace and chimney
- Secure and properly functioning components like the damper, cap, and crown
- Safe and efficient operation of the fireplace and any associated accessories

By catching and correcting these issues early, you can help prevent more serious and costly problems down the road, as well as ensure the safe and efficient operation of your fireplace.

2. Chimney Sweeping:

Another key task that is best left to the professionals is chimney sweeping. While some homeowners may be tempted to tackle this job themselves with DIY tools and methods, the reality is that proper chimney sweeping requires specialized equipment, training, and expertise to do safely and effectively.

During a professional chimney sweeping, a certified technician will use a variety of brushes, rods, and vacuums to remove creosote, soot, and other debris from the entire length of your flue and chimney. They will also inspect the system for any signs of damage or deterioration, and make recommendations for any necessary repairs or maintenance.

Depending on factors like the type and frequency of use, most chimneys should be professionally swept at least once a year, and more often if you burn a lot of wood or notice any signs of poor performance or excessive smoke.

3. Major Repairs:

If you notice any significant damage or performance issues with your fireplace or chimney, it's always best to call in a professional for an assessment and repair. Attempting to tackle major repairs yourself can be dangerous and may even make the problem worse if not done properly.

Some common fireplace and chimney issues that require professional attention include:

- Cracks or gaps in the chimney structure or lining
- Damaged or missing components like the cap, crown, or damper
- Leaks or moisture intrusion in the chimney or fireplace
- Excessive creosote buildup or other blockages in the flue
- Malfunctioning or inefficient fireplace inserts or gas logs

A qualified fireplace and chimney technician will have the tools, knowledge, and experience needed to properly diagnose and repair these issues, ensuring the safety and performance of your system.

4. Gas Fireplace Installation and Maintenance:
If you have a gas fireplace or are considering installing one, it's especially important to work with licensed and certified professionals for all installation and maintenance needs. Gas fireplaces involve complex fuel lines, valves, and other components that require specialized knowledge and tools to work with safely and effectively.

During a gas fireplace installation, a professional will typically:

- Assess your space and heating needs to recommend an appropriate fireplace size and style
- Install and connect the necessary gas lines, valves, and other components according to local codes and manufacturer specifications
- Test and calibrate the fireplace and any associated controls or accessories for safe and efficient operation
- Provide guidance on proper use and maintenance to ensure long-term performance and safety

Similarly, for ongoing maintenance and repairs of gas fireplaces, it's always best to work with a licensed and experienced technician who can properly diagnose and address any issues with the fuel lines, ignition system, or other key components.

5. Chimney Relining:

Another complex and high-stakes job that is best left to the professionals is chimney relining. Over time, the lining of your chimney can become damaged or deteriorated due to factors like age, moisture, and excessive heat, which can compromise the safety and efficiency of your fireplace.

If your chimney needs relining, a professional will typically:

- Assess the condition of your existing lining and recommend an appropriate relining material and method
- Remove any damaged or deteriorated lining material and prepare the chimney for the new liner
- Install the new lining material according to manufacturer specifications and local codes, ensuring a secure and properly sized fit
- Test and inspect the new lining to ensure safe and efficient operation of the fireplace and chimney

Attempting to reline a chimney yourself can be extremely dangerous and may even void your homeowners insurance or violate local building codes, so it's always best to leave this job to the experts.

DIY Fireplace Care:

While there are certainly many fireplace and chimney tasks that require professional attention, there are also some basic maintenance and care tasks that homeowners can often handle themselves with the right tools and knowledge. These may include:

- Regular cleaning of the firebox, grate, and other interior components
- Periodic checks for obvious damage or performance issues
- Proper storage and seasoning of firewood
- Safe and appropriate use of fireplace tools and accessories
- Basic troubleshooting and adjustments of gas fireplace controls or components

By staying on top of these routine tasks and knowing when to call in the pros for more complex or high-stakes jobs, you can help ensure the longevity, safety, and performance of your fireplace for years to come.

Ultimately, the decision between hiring professionals and tackling fireplace care yourself will depend on factors like your level of expertise, comfort with tools and safety protocols, and the complexity and risk of the task at hand. When in doubt, it's always better to err on the side of caution and work with a qualified and experienced professional to ensure the best possible outcome for your fireplace and home.

What to look for when hiring fireplace contractors

When it comes to ensuring the safety, performance, and longevity of your fireplace and chimney, hiring the right contractor is essential. However, with so many options out there, it can be challenging to know what to look for and how to choose the best professional for your needs. In this section, we'll explore some key factors to consider when hiring fireplace contractors, so you can make an informed decision and get the best possible service for your home.

1. Certification and Licensing:

One of the first and most important things to look for when hiring a fireplace contractor is proper certification and licensing. In most states, fireplace and chimney professionals are required to hold certain certifications and licenses to operate legally and safely. These may include:

- Chimney Safety Institute of America (CSIA) certification
- National Fireplace Institute (NFI) certification
- EPA certification for wood-burning appliances
- State or local business licenses and permits

When researching potential contractors, be sure to ask about their specific certifications and licenses, and verify them with the appropriate organizations or agencies. A reputable and qualified contractor should be happy to provide proof of their credentials and explain their relevance to your project.

2. Insurance and Liability:

Another critical factor to consider when hiring a fireplace contractor is insurance and liability coverage. Even with the best training and safety protocols, accidents and injuries can still happen on the job. If your contractor doesn't have adequate insurance coverage, you could be held liable for any damages or injuries that occur on your property.

When interviewing potential contractors, be sure to ask about their insurance policies and coverage limits, and request proof of insurance before signing any contracts. A reputable contractor should carry both general liability and workers' compensation insurance to protect themselves and their clients.

3. Experience and Expertise:

When it comes to complex and potentially hazardous systems like fireplaces and chimneys, experience and expertise are essential. While a newly certified contractor may be knowledgeable and skilled, there's no substitute for real-world experience and a proven track record of success.

When researching potential contractors, look for professionals with several years of experience in the specific services you need, whether that's chimney sweeping, gas fireplace installation, or masonry repair. Ask about their training, certifications, and past projects, and look for examples of their work or testimonials from previous clients.

4. Professionalism and Customer Service:

In addition to technical expertise and experience, it's also important to consider a contractor's professionalism and customer service when making your hiring decision. After all, you'll be working closely with this person or team throughout your project, and you want to feel confident and comfortable with their communication, reliability, and overall approach.

When interviewing potential contractors, pay attention to factors like:

- Promptness and responsiveness to your inquiries and requests
- Clarity and thoroughness in explaining their services, pricing, and process

- Willingness to answer your questions and address your concerns
- Respectfulness and courteousness in their interactions with you and your family
- Attention to detail and commitment to quality in their work and customer service

A reputable and professional contractor should be easy to communicate with, transparent about their services and pricing, and dedicated to ensuring your satisfaction and safety throughout the project.

5. References and Reviews:

One of the best ways to gauge a fireplace contractor's quality and reliability is to hear from their previous clients. When researching potential contractors, be sure to ask for references or testimonials from past customers, and take the time to follow up and ask about their experiences.

Some key questions to ask references may include:

- How satisfied were you with the contractor's work and customer service?
- Did the project stay on schedule and within budget?
- Were there any issues or concerns that arose during the project, and how did the contractor handle them?
- Would you hire this contractor again or recommend them to others?

In addition to personal references, you can also look for online reviews and ratings on sites like Yelp, Google, or the Better Business Bureau. While no contractor will have perfect reviews across the board, a pattern of positive feedback and satisfied customers can be a good sign of their quality and reliability.

6. Detailed Estimates and Contracts:

Finally, when hiring a fireplace contractor, it's important to get detailed, written estimates and contracts before any work begins. A reputable contractor should be happy to provide a clear and thorough breakdown of their services, materials, and pricing, as well as a timeline for the project and any contingencies or warranties.

When reviewing estimates and contracts, be sure to look for:

- Detailed descriptions of the work to be performed and materials to be used
- Itemized pricing for each component of the project
- Estimated start and completion dates
- Payment terms and schedules
- Any warranties or guarantees on the work or materials
- Any permits or inspections required for the project

If a contractor is hesitant to provide detailed estimates or contracts, or if their pricing seems too good to be true, it may be a red flag for potential issues down the road.

By considering these key factors and doing your due diligence when researching and interviewing potential fireplace contractors, you can find a professional who will provide the expertise, quality, and customer service you need to keep your fireplace and chimney safe and functional for years to come. Remember, when it comes to complex and critical systems like these, it's always better to invest in hiring the right professional than to cut corners and risk costly or dangerous consequences down the road.

Fireplace and chimney care tasks you can handle yourself

While many fireplace and chimney maintenance tasks are best left to trained professionals, there are still several important care and upkeep tasks that homeowners can often handle themselves with the right tools, knowledge, and safety precautions. By staying on top of these DIY tasks, you can help prolong the life and performance of your fireplace and chimney, while also catching potential issues early and knowing when to call in the pros. In this section, we'll explore some of the key fireplace and chimney care tasks you can handle yourself, along with step-by-step instructions and important safety considerations.

1. Regular Cleaning:
One of the most important and accessible fireplace and chimney care tasks you can handle yourself is regular cleaning. By removing soot, ash, and debris from your fireplace and chimney components on a consistent basis, you can help prevent buildup and blockages that can affect performance and safety over time.

Some key cleaning tasks to handle yourself may include:

- Removing ashes and debris from the firebox after each use, using a metal scoop and ash bucket.
- Brushing or vacuuming the interior of the firebox, grate, and other components to remove soot and residue.
- Wiping down the exterior of the fireplace and mantel with a damp cloth to remove dust and grime.
- Cleaning the glass doors or screen with a specialized cleaner and soft cloth to maintain visibility and performance.

When cleaning your fireplace and chimney components, always make sure the system is completely cool and use appropriate tools and safety gear, such as gloves, goggles, and a dust mask. Avoid using harsh chemicals or abrasive materials that could damage the components or create hazardous fumes.

2. Visual Inspections:

Another important DIY task for fireplace and chimney care is regular visual inspections. By taking the time to carefully examine your fireplace and chimney components on a consistent basis, you can catch potential issues early and know when to call in a professional for a more thorough assessment.

Some key areas to visually inspect may include:

- The firebox and grate for cracks, gaps, or other damage.
- The damper and flue for proper operation and any signs of obstruction or damage.
- The chimney exterior for cracks, spalling, or other signs of deterioration.
- The chimney cap and crown for proper fit and any signs of rust, damage, or debris.
- The roof and attic area around the chimney for any signs of leaks, moisture, or other damage.

When conducting visual inspections, use a bright flashlight and take your time to examine each component carefully. If you notice any significant damage, obstruction, or other concerns, it's best to call in a professional for a more thorough assessment and any necessary repairs.

3. Proper Fuel Selection and Storage:

If you have a wood-burning fireplace, another important DIY task is selecting and storing your fuel properly. By choosing the right firewood and storing it correctly, you can help ensure a cleaner, more efficient burn and reduce the risk of chimney fires and other hazards.

When selecting firewood, look for dense hardwoods like oak, hickory, or maple that have been properly seasoned for at least six months to a year. Avoid softwoods like pine or cedar, which can create more creosote buildup in your chimney, as well as any wood that is green, moldy, or infested with insects.

When storing firewood, keep it stacked neatly in a dry, covered area at least 30 feet away from your home and any other structures. Avoid storing wood directly on the ground, which can promote moisture and insect infestation, and rotate your stock regularly to use the oldest and driest wood first.

4. Safe and Efficient Operation:

Another key DIY task for fireplace and chimney care is ensuring the safe and efficient operation of your system. By following best practices for building, tending, and extinguishing your fires, you can help minimize safety risks and maximize the performance and enjoyment of your fireplace.

Some key tips for safe and efficient fireplace operation may include:

- Opening the damper fully before starting a fire and keeping it open until the fire is completely extinguished.
- Using a small amount of dry kindling and newspaper to start the fire, and gradually adding larger logs as it builds.

- Keeping the fire small and manageable, and avoiding overloading the firebox or letting the flames get too high.
- Using fireplace tools like a poker, tongs, and shovel to tend the fire safely and efficiently.
- Allowing the fire to burn out completely before closing the damper and retiring for the night.
- Disposing of ashes in a metal container with a tight-fitting lid, and storing them outside your home until completely cool.

By following these tips and staying vigilant about the safety and performance of your fireplace, you can enjoy cozy, efficient fires all season long.

5. Knowing When to Call in the Pros:
Finally, one of the most important DIY tasks for fireplace and chimney care is knowing when to call in the professionals. Even if you're diligent about cleaning, inspecting, and operating your fireplace safely, there are still some tasks and issues that require specialized expertise and tools to handle properly.

Some key signs that it's time to call in a professional may include:

- Significant buildup of creosote or other debris in your chimney that you can't remove yourself.
- Cracks, gaps, or other damage to your firebox, flue, or chimney that could affect safety or performance.
- Strange odors, sounds, or behavior from your fireplace or chimney that you can't identify or resolve.
- Difficulty starting or maintaining a fire, or excessive smoke or sparks coming into your living space.
- Annual inspections and cleanings, which are best left to trained and certified professionals.

If you notice any of these signs or have any doubts about the safety or performance of your fireplace and chimney, don't hesitate to call in a reputable and qualified professional. The peace of mind and protection for your home and family are well worth the investment.

By staying on top of these key DIY tasks and knowing when to call in the pros, you can help ensure the longevity, safety, and performance of your fireplace and chimney for years to come. Just remember to always prioritize safety and follow best practices for cleaning, maintenance, and operation, and don't hesitate to seek professional guidance when needed.

Chapter 6
Fireplace and Chimney Safety Essentials

Fire safety musts for operating fireplaces

While fireplaces can provide warmth, ambiance, and enjoyment for your home, they also come with inherent safety risks that require vigilance and proactive measures to mitigate. From the risk of chimney fires and carbon monoxide poisoning to burns and property damage, there are several key safety essentials that every fireplace owner should know and follow. In this section, we'll explore some of the most critical fire safety musts for operating fireplaces, along with tips and best practices for ensuring a safe and enjoyable fireplace experience.

Fire Safety Musts for Operating Fireplaces:

1. Annual Inspections and Cleanings:
One of the most important fire safety musts for operating fireplaces is scheduling annual inspections and cleanings with a qualified professional. Even if you're diligent about cleaning and maintaining your fireplace yourself, there are still many potential hazards and issues that require specialized expertise and tools to identify and address.

During an annual inspection and cleaning, a certified chimney sweep will typically:

- Inspect the entire fireplace and chimney system for any cracks, damage, or obstructions.
- Clean the chimney flue and other components to remove creosote, soot, and debris buildup.
- Check the damper, cap, and other components for proper operation and fit.

- Assess the overall safety and performance of the system and recommend any necessary repairs or upgrades.

By scheduling these professional services annually, you can catch potential safety hazards early, ensure optimal performance and efficiency, and have peace of mind knowing your fireplace is in good hands.

2. Proper Fuel Selection and Use:

Another critical fire safety must for operating fireplaces is using the proper fuel and burning it correctly. Whether you have a wood-burning, gas, or electric fireplace, it's important to follow manufacturer guidelines and best practices for fuel selection and use to minimize safety risks and maximize performance.

For wood-burning fireplaces, this means:

- Using only properly seasoned hardwood that has been split and stored for at least six months.
- Avoiding softwoods, treated wood, or any other materials that can create excessive smoke or hazardous fumes.
- Building small, hot fires rather than large, smoldering ones to minimize creosote buildup and other hazards.
- Never using accelerants like gasoline, kerosene, or lighter fluid to start or enhance a fire.

For gas fireplaces, this means:

- Using only the fuel type and grade specified by the manufacturer, such as natural gas or propane.
- Having the gas lines and connections professionally installed and inspected for leaks and proper operation.
- Keeping the burner and other components clean and free of debris or obstructions.

- Never using the fireplace if you smell gas or suspect a leak, and contacting a professional immediately.

For electric fireplaces, this means:

- Using only the specified wattage and type of bulbs or heating elements.
- Keeping the fireplace and its components clean and free of dust, debris, or obstructions.
- Never using the fireplace if you notice any frayed wires, sparks, or other signs of electrical malfunction.

By following these fuel selection and use guidelines, you can help ensure a safer and more efficient fireplace experience.

3. Safe and Proper Operation:
In addition to proper fuel selection and use, it's also important to follow safe and proper operating procedures for your fireplace to minimize risks and maximize enjoyment. This includes:

- Always opening the damper fully before starting a fire and keeping it open until the fire is completely extinguished.
- Using a fireplace screen or glass doors to prevent sparks, embers, or logs from escaping the firebox.
- Keeping any flammable materials like furniture, curtains, or décor at least three feet away from the fireplace.
- Never leaving a fire unattended or allowing it to burn overnight or while you're away from home.
- Keeping a fire extinguisher, smoke detector, and carbon monoxide detector in good working order and easily accessible near the fireplace.
- Teaching all family members and guests about fireplace safety and supervising children and pets closely around the fire.

By following these safe operating procedures and staying vigilant about the condition and performance of your fireplace, you can enjoy cozy and warm fires with greater peace of mind.

4. Regular Cleaning and Maintenance:

Another key fire safety must for operating fireplaces is staying on top of regular cleaning and maintenance tasks. Even with annual professional inspections and cleanings, there are still several important upkeep tasks that homeowners should handle themselves to minimize safety risks and ensure optimal performance.

These tasks may include:
- Regularly removing ashes and debris from the firebox and disposing of them in a metal container outside the home.
- Cleaning the glass doors or screen with a specialized cleaner and soft cloth to maintain visibility and performance.
- Inspecting the firebox, damper, and other components for any signs of damage, deterioration, or malfunction.
- Keeping the area around the fireplace clean and free of clutter or combustible materials.
- Checking the batteries in smoke and carbon monoxide detectors and replacing them as needed.

By staying diligent about these cleaning and maintenance tasks, you can help catch potential safety hazards early, prolong the life and performance of your fireplace, and ensure a more enjoyable and worry-free experience.

5. Knowing When to Call a Professional:

Finally, one of the most important fire safety musts for operating fireplaces is knowing when to call in a professional for assistance. Even if you're confident in your ability to clean, maintain, and operate your fireplace safely, there are still some issues and tasks that require specialized expertise and tools to handle properly.

Some key signs that it's time to call a professional may include:

- Persistent or excessive smoke, sparks, or fumes coming from the fireplace or chimney.
- Strange odors, sounds, or behavior from the fireplace that you can't identify or resolve.
- Visible damage or deterioration to the firebox, damper, flue, or other components.
- Difficulty starting or maintaining a fire, or poor overall performance and efficiency.
- Any doubts or concerns about the safety or integrity of your fireplace or chimney system.

If you notice any of these signs or have any other reasons to suspect a problem with your fireplace, don't hesitate to call a certified chimney sweep or fireplace professional for an inspection and any necessary repairs or maintenance. The safety and protection of your home and family are always worth the investment.

By following these fire safety musts and staying proactive about the care and operation of your fireplace, you can enjoy all the benefits and pleasures of a cozy fire with greater confidence and peace of mind. Remember, when it comes to fireplace safety, an ounce of prevention is truly worth a pound of cure.

Chimney and vent safety considerations

In addition to the fire safety essentials for operating fireplaces, there are also several critical safety considerations specific to chimneys and vents that every homeowner should be aware of. From the risk of carbon monoxide poisoning and chimney fires to structural damage and performance issues, chimneys and vents play a vital role in the safety and efficiency of your fireplace system. In this section, we'll explore some of the key chimney and vent safety considerations to keep in mind, along with tips and best practices for ensuring optimal performance and longevity.

1. Carbon Monoxide Risks:

One of the most serious safety risks associated with chimneys and vents is the potential for carbon monoxide (CO) poisoning. Carbon monoxide is a colorless, odorless, and tasteless gas that can be produced by any fuel-burning appliance, including fireplaces, when there is incomplete combustion or inadequate ventilation.

If your chimney or vent is blocked, damaged, or improperly sized, it can allow CO to build up inside your home, leading to potentially deadly consequences. Some common signs of CO buildup may include:

- Flu-like symptoms such as headaches, dizziness, nausea, and fatigue.
- Soot or brownish-yellow stains around the fireplace or on the walls or ceiling.
- Pilot lights or burner flames that are mostly yellow rather than blue.
- Excessive moisture or condensation on windows or walls near the fireplace.

To minimize the risk of CO poisoning from your fireplace and chimney, it's important to:

- Have your chimney and vent professionally inspected and cleaned at least once a year to ensure proper sizing, performance, and safety.
- Install and regularly test carbon monoxide detectors on every level of your home and near any fuel-burning appliances, including fireplaces.
- Never use your fireplace if you suspect a problem with the chimney or vent, such as blockages, damage, or inadequate draft.
- Always open the damper fully before starting a fire and keep it open until the fire is completely extinguished.
- Never use your fireplace as a primary heat source or leave it burning unattended or overnight.

By taking these precautions and staying vigilant about the safety and performance of your chimney and vent, you can help protect your home and family from the dangers of CO poisoning.

2. Chimney Fire Risks:
Another serious safety risk associated with chimneys and vents is the potential for chimney fires. Chimney fires occur when the buildup of creosote or other flammable residues inside the chimney ignites, creating a fast-moving and potentially destructive blaze.

Some common causes of chimney fires may include:
- Infrequent or inadequate chimney cleanings, allowing creosote and other residues to accumulate.
- Using unseasoned or inappropriate firewood that produces more smoke and creosote.
- Overloading the fireplace or allowing fires to smolder or burn too slowly, increasing creosote production.

- Cracks, gaps, or other damage to the chimney liner or masonry that allow heat and sparks to escape.

To minimize the risk of chimney fires, it's important to:

- Have your chimney professionally cleaned and inspected at least once a year, or more often if you use your fireplace frequently.
- Use only properly seasoned hardwood and build small, hot fires rather than large, smoldering ones.
- Never burn cardboard, wrapping paper, or other inappropriate materials that can spark and ignite creosote.
- Repair any cracks, gaps, or other damage to your chimney promptly to prevent heat and sparks from escaping.
- Never use flammable liquids or accelerants to start or enhance a fire in your fireplace.

If you do experience a chimney fire, it's important to call 911 immediately and evacuate your home until the fire is fully extinguished and the chimney is inspected for damage. Even a small or short-lived chimney fire can cause significant damage to your chimney and home, so it's always better to err on the side of caution.

3. Structural Damage Risks:

In addition to the risks of CO poisoning and chimney fires, chimneys and vents can also pose structural damage risks to your home if they are not properly maintained and repaired. Over time, exposure to heat, moisture, and other elements can cause chimneys and vents to deteriorate, leading to cracks, leaks, and other damage that can compromise the safety and integrity of your home.

Some common signs of chimney or vent structural damage may include:

- Cracks or gaps in the chimney masonry or flue liner.
- Leaning, tilting, or separating of the chimney structure from the home.
- Moisture stains or damage on the ceiling, walls, or floor around the fireplace or chimney.
- Flaking, spalling, or crumbling of the chimney bricks or mortar.
- Rusting or corrosion of the chimney cap, damper, or other metal components.

To minimize the risk of structural damage to your chimney and home, it's important to:

- Have your chimney and vent professionally inspected at least once a year to identify and address any signs of damage or deterioration early.
- Repair any cracks, gaps, or other damage to the chimney promptly to prevent moisture intrusion and further deterioration.
- Install a chimney cap and keep it in good repair to prevent water, debris, and animals from entering and damaging the chimney.
- Maintain proper clearance between the chimney and any nearby trees, buildings, or other structures to prevent damage from falling limbs or shifting foundations.
- Address any signs of moisture damage or leaks around the chimney promptly to prevent rot, mold, and other structural issues.

By staying proactive about the inspection, maintenance, and repair of your chimney and vent, you can help prevent costly and potentially dangerous structural damage to your home.

4. Performance and Efficiency Considerations:

Finally, in addition to the safety considerations, there are also several important performance and efficiency factors to keep in mind when it comes to chimneys and vents. Even if your chimney and vent are structurally sound and free of safety hazards, they may still be underperforming or operating inefficiently due to issues like improper sizing, inadequate height, or poor design.

Some common signs of chimney or vent performance issues may include:

- Difficulty starting or maintaining a fire in your fireplace.
- Excessive smoke or odors coming into your home from the fireplace.
- Poor draft or airflow up the chimney, leading to incomplete combustion and creosote buildup.
- Condensation or moisture buildup inside the chimney or fireplace.
- Higher than normal heating bills or reduced heat output from the fireplace.

To optimize the performance and efficiency of your chimney and vent, it's important to:

- Have your chimney and vent professionally inspected and evaluated to ensure proper sizing, height, and design for your specific fireplace and home.
- Address any performance issues promptly to prevent further damage or inefficiency, such as installing a chimney liner or modifying the fireplace opening.
- Use proper fuel and burning techniques to maximize heat output and minimize creosote and other byproducts.
- Keep the chimney and fireplace clean and well-maintained to ensure optimal airflow and combustion.

- Consider upgrading to a more efficient fireplace or insert if your current system is underperforming or no longer meeting your needs.

By taking these steps to optimize the performance and efficiency of your chimney and vent, you can enjoy a warmer, more comfortable home while also saving money on your heating bills and minimizing your environmental impact.

In conclusion, chimneys and vents are critical components of any fireplace system, and their safety, performance, and longevity should never be taken for granted. By understanding the key safety considerations and best practices outlined in this section, and staying proactive about inspection, maintenance, and repair, you can enjoy all the benefits of a cozy fireplace with greater peace of mind and confidence. Remember, when it comes to chimney and vent safety, an ounce of prevention is always worth a pound of cure.

Childproofing and preventing accidents around fireplaces

Fireplaces can be a beautiful and cozy addition to any home, but they also pose significant safety risks, especially for young children and pets. From the risk of burns and smoke inhalation to the dangers of fire and carbon monoxide poisoning, it's essential for homeowners with fireplaces to take proactive steps to childproof their homes and prevent accidents. In this section, we'll explore some key strategies and best practices for childproofing and preventing accidents around fireplaces, so you can enjoy the warmth and ambiance of your fireplace with greater peace of mind and safety.

1. Install a Fireplace Screen or Gate:
One of the most effective ways to childproof your fireplace and prevent accidents is to install a fireplace screen or gate. A fireplace screen is a mesh or glass barrier that fits over the fireplace opening, preventing sparks, embers, and logs from escaping while still allowing heat and light to pass through. A fireplace gate, on the other hand, is a freestanding barrier that can be placed around the entire fireplace area, creating a safe zone that children and pets cannot enter.

When choosing a fireplace screen or gate, look for products that are:
- Sturdy and durable, able to withstand the heat and wear and tear of regular use.
- Properly sized and fitted for your specific fireplace opening or area.
- Easy to install and remove as needed for cleaning and maintenance.
- Designed with child safety features such as secure latches, rounded corners, and non-toxic finishes.

By installing a high-quality fireplace screen or gate, you can create an effective barrier between your children and the dangers of the fireplace, while still enjoying the warmth and ambiance of the fire.

2. Establish and Enforce Fireplace Safety Rules:

Another important aspect of childproofing and preventing accidents around fireplaces is establishing and enforcing clear safety rules for your family and any visitors to your home. Some key fireplace safety rules to consider include:

- Never leave children or pets unattended around a burning fireplace.
- Keep all flammable objects, such as paper, blankets, and toys, at least three feet away from the fireplace.
- Never touch the glass, screen, or metal surfaces of the fireplace, as they can become extremely hot and cause severe burns.
- Never throw anything into the fireplace, such as toys, trash, or other objects that can catch fire or release toxic fumes.
- Always keep the fireplace area clear of clutter and debris, and store fireplace tools and accessories out of reach of children.

To reinforce these safety rules, consider:
- Discussing fireplace safety with your children regularly and modeling safe behavior yourself.
- Posting written safety rules near the fireplace as a visual reminder.
- Praising and rewarding your children for following fireplace safety rules consistently.
- Establishing clear consequences for violating fireplace safety rules, such as loss of fireplace privileges or extra supervision.

By establishing and enforcing clear fireplace safety rules, you can help create a culture of safety in your home and reduce the risk of accidents and injuries.

3. Store Fireplace Tools and Accessories Safely:
Fireplace tools and accessories, such as pokers, tongs, and matches, can be dangerous in the hands of curious children. To prevent accidents and injuries, it's important to store these items safely and securely out of reach of children. Some tips for storing fireplace tools and accessories safely include:

- Keeping all tools and accessories in a locked cabinet or drawer when not in use.
- Storing matches and lighters in a high, out-of-reach location, such as a top shelf or lockbox.
- Using a fireplace tool stand or rack to keep tools organized and secure near the fireplace, but out of reach of children.
- Never leaving tools or accessories lying around the fireplace area where children can access them.

By storing fireplace tools and accessories safely and securely, you can help prevent accidents and keep your children safe around the fireplace.

4. Educate Your Children About Fireplace Safety:
In addition to establishing and enforcing safety rules, it's also important to educate your children about the dangers of fireplaces and how to stay safe around them. Some key topics to cover in your fireplace safety education include:

- The difference between a "hot" fireplace and a "cold" fireplace, and how to tell when it's safe to be near the fireplace.
- The importance of never touching or getting too close to the fireplace, even if it looks like the fire is out.
- What to do in case of a fire emergency, such as calling 911 and evacuating the home safely.
- The dangers of carbon monoxide and how to recognize the signs of CO poisoning, such as headaches, dizziness, and nausea.

To make your fireplace safety education more engaging and effective, consider:

- Using age-appropriate language and examples to explain fireplace safety concepts.
- Incorporating hands-on demonstrations or role-playing exercises to reinforce key safety messages.
- Using visual aids such as videos, books, or posters to illustrate fireplace safety principles.
- Encouraging your children to ask questions and share their own ideas about fireplace safety.

By educating your children about fireplace safety in a clear, consistent, and engaging way, you can help them develop the knowledge and skills they need to stay safe around fireplaces throughout their lives.

5. Maintain Your Fireplace and Chimney Regularly:
Finally, one of the most important steps you can take to prevent accidents and ensure the safety of your children around fireplaces is to maintain your fireplace and chimney regularly. A poorly maintained fireplace and chimney can pose serious risks, such as chimney fires, carbon monoxide leaks, and structural damage, which can put your entire family at risk.

To maintain your fireplace and chimney properly, be sure to:

- Have your fireplace and chimney professionally inspected and cleaned at least once a year, or more often if you use your fireplace frequently.
- Repair any cracks, gaps, or other damage to your fireplace or chimney promptly to prevent further deterioration and safety hazards.

- Use only properly seasoned hardwood in your fireplace, and avoid burning trash, paper, or other inappropriate materials that can spark or release toxic fumes.
- Keep the area around your fireplace clean and free of debris, and dispose of ashes and other waste properly in a metal container with a tight-fitting lid.
- Install and maintain smoke and carbon monoxide detectors on every level of your home, and test them regularly to ensure they are working properly.

By maintaining your fireplace and chimney regularly and taking proactive steps to ensure their safety and performance, you can create a safer and more comfortable environment for your entire family, including your children and pets.

In conclusion, childproofing and preventing accidents around fireplaces is an essential responsibility for any homeowner with young children or pets. By installing safety barriers, establishing and enforcing safety rules, storing tools and accessories securely, educating your children about fireplace safety, and maintaining your fireplace and chimney regularly, you can significantly reduce the risk of accidents and injuries and enjoy the warmth and beauty of your fireplace with greater peace of mind. Remember, when it comes to fireplace safety, prevention is always the best policy.

Chapter 7
Upgrading, Converting or Adding a Fireplace

Options for updating an old fireplace

If you have an old, inefficient, or unattractive fireplace in your home, or if you're considering adding a new fireplace to enhance your home's ambiance and value, there are many options available for upgrading, converting, or adding a fireplace. From simple cosmetic updates to full-scale renovations, the possibilities are endless when it comes to transforming your fireplace and creating the cozy, inviting space you've always wanted. In this section, we'll explore some of the most popular options for updating an old fireplace, as well as some key considerations and best practices for upgrading, converting, or adding a fireplace to your home.

Options for Updating an Old Fireplace:

1. Cosmetic Updates:

If your old fireplace is structurally sound but looking a bit dated or drab, there are many simple cosmetic updates you can make to give it a fresh, modern look. Some popular options for cosmetic fireplace updates include:

- Painting or whitewashing the brick or stone to create a cleaner, brighter look.
- Adding new tiles or stone veneer to the surround or hearth to update the color and texture.
- Installing a new mantel or shelving to create a focal point and display space.
- Updating the fireplace screen or doors with a new design or finish.
- Adding new lighting or accessories to enhance the ambiance and style of the fireplace.

When making cosmetic updates to your old fireplace, be sure to:

- Choose materials and finishes that complement the overall style and decor of your home.
- Consider the scale and proportion of your fireplace in relation to the room and any new elements you add.
- Hire a professional to handle any structural or safety-related updates, such as installing a new hearth or relining the chimney.
- Test any paint or finish on a small, inconspicuous area before applying it to the entire fireplace to ensure compatibility and adhesion.

By making simple cosmetic updates to your old fireplace, you can give it a whole new look and feel without the expense or hassle of a full-scale renovation.

2. Fireplace Inserts:

If your old fireplace is inefficient, drafty, or difficult to use, installing a fireplace insert can be a great way to update its performance and functionality. A fireplace insert is essentially a self-contained unit that fits inside your existing fireplace and provides a more efficient, controllable, and attractive heating option.

There are several types of fireplace inserts available, including:

- Gas inserts: These inserts use natural gas or propane to create a realistic flame and heat output, with the convenience of a remote control or wall switch.
- Electric inserts: These inserts use electricity to create a simulated flame and heat output, with no need for venting or fuel lines.

- Wood-burning inserts: These inserts are designed to burn wood more efficiently and cleanly than a traditional open fireplace, with features like air-tight doors and secondary combustion.
- Pellet inserts: These inserts burn compressed wood or biomass pellets to create a consistent, efficient heat output, with automated feeding and temperature control.

When choosing a fireplace insert, be sure to:

- Consider your heating needs and preferences, as well as the size and layout of your existing fireplace and home.
- Look for inserts with high efficiency ratings and low emissions, to maximize your energy savings and minimize your environmental impact.
- Hire a professional to handle the installation and any necessary chimney or venting modifications, to ensure safety and performance.
- Consider the aesthetics of the insert and how it will integrate with your existing fireplace and decor.

By installing a fireplace insert, you can update the performance, efficiency, and convenience of your old fireplace, while also enhancing its visual appeal and comfort.

3. Full-Scale Renovation:
If your old fireplace is beyond repair or no longer meets your needs and preferences, a full-scale renovation may be the best option for updating and upgrading your fireplace. A full-scale fireplace renovation involves removing the old fireplace and replacing it with a new one, either in the same location or in a different part of your home.

Some popular options for full-scale fireplace renovations include:
- Converting a traditional wood-burning fireplace to a gas or electric model for greater convenience and efficiency.
- Replacing an old, inefficient masonry fireplace with a new, high-efficiency prefabricated or zero-clearance model.
- Adding a new fireplace to a room that doesn't currently have one, such as a basement, bedroom, or outdoor living space.
- Redesigning the entire fireplace wall or surround to create a new focal point and style for your home.

When planning a full-scale fireplace renovation, be sure to:
- Consult with a professional fireplace installer or contractor to assess your home's structure, venting, and fuel options, and to ensure compliance with local building codes and safety standards.
- Consider your lifestyle, heating needs, and design preferences when selecting a new fireplace type, size, and location.
- Plan for any necessary electrical, gas, or chimney modifications, and factor these costs into your overall renovation budget.
- Choose materials, finishes, and accessories that complement your home's architecture and decor, and that will stand up to the heat and wear of regular use.

By undertaking a full-scale fireplace renovation, you can completely transform the look, feel, and functionality of your fireplace and create a stunning new focal point for your home.

4. Converting to a Different Fuel Source:

If you're looking to update your old fireplace for greater efficiency, convenience, or environmental friendliness, converting to a different fuel source may be a good option. The most common fireplace fuel conversions are from wood-burning to gas or electric, but there are also options for converting from gas to wood or pellets, or from electric to gas.

When considering a fireplace fuel conversion, be sure to:

- Assess your home's existing fuel sources and lines, and determine whether any new lines or hookups will be needed for the conversion.
- Consider the cost and availability of the new fuel source in your area, as well as any ongoing maintenance or safety requirements.
- Hire a professional to handle the conversion and any necessary chimney or venting modifications, to ensure safety and performance.
- Choose a new fireplace or insert that is compatible with your existing fireplace opening and structure, and that meets your heating and design needs.

Some benefits of converting to a different fireplace fuel source include:

- Increased efficiency and heat output, particularly with gas or pellet models.
- Greater convenience and control, with features like remote ignition, thermostatic control, and programmable settings.
- Reduced environmental impact and indoor air pollution, particularly with electric or gas models.
- Enhanced safety and peace of mind, with features like automatic shut-off, sealed combustion, and direct venting.

By converting your old fireplace to a different fuel source, you can update its performance, convenience, and environmental friendliness, while also potentially increasing your home's value and marketability.

Adding a New Fireplace:

If you're considering adding a new fireplace to your home, either in addition to or instead of an existing one, there are many options and considerations to keep in mind. Adding a new fireplace can enhance your home's ambiance, comfort, and value, but it also requires careful planning and execution to ensure safety, performance, and aesthetics.

Some popular options for adding a new fireplace to your home include:

- Installing a traditional wood-burning fireplace in a new location, such as a basement or outdoor living space.
- Adding a gas or electric fireplace to a room that doesn't currently have one, such as a bedroom or home office.
- Incorporating a fireplace into a new home addition or renovation, such as a sunroom or master suite.
- Creating a double-sided or multi-sided fireplace that can be enjoyed from multiple rooms or angles.

When adding a new fireplace to your home, be sure to:

- Consult with a professional fireplace installer or contractor to assess your home's structure, venting, and fuel options, and to ensure compliance with local building codes and safety standards.
- Consider the size, style, and location of the new fireplace in relation to your home's layout, decor, and heating needs.
- Plan for any necessary electrical, gas, or chimney installations or modifications, and factor these costs into your overall project budget.
- Choose materials, finishes, and accessories that complement your home's architecture and style, and that will provide lasting beauty and performance.

- Ensure proper ventilation and safety features are installed, such as chimney liners, caps, and carbon monoxide detectors.

By carefully planning and executing the addition of a new fireplace to your home, you can create a stunning new focal point and gathering space that will provide warmth, comfort, and enjoyment for years to come.

Conclusion:
Whether you're looking to update an old fireplace, convert to a different fuel source, or add a new fireplace to your home, there are many options and considerations to keep in mind. From simple cosmetic updates to full-scale renovations, the possibilities for upgrading and enhancing your fireplace are endless. By working with a professional installer or contractor, carefully assessing your needs and preferences, and choosing high-quality materials and accessories, you can create a fireplace that is safe, efficient, and beautiful, and that will provide lasting value and enjoyment for your home and family.

Converting from wood-burning to gas (or vice versa)

If you're considering converting your wood-burning fireplace to gas or your gas fireplace to wood-burning, there are several factors to consider before making the switch. Both options have their pros and cons, and the best choice for you will depend on your specific needs, preferences, and home setup. In this section, we'll explore the key considerations and steps involved in converting from wood-burning to gas and vice versa, so you can make an informed decision and ensure a safe and successful conversion.

Converting from Wood-Burning to Gas:

One of the most popular fireplace conversions is from wood-burning to gas. Gas fireplaces offer several benefits over traditional wood-burning models, including:

- Greater convenience and ease of use, with no need to chop, store, or haul firewood.
- Cleaner and more efficient burning, with less smoke, ash, and creosote buildup.
- More consistent and controllable heat output, with options for thermostatic control and remote operation.
- Enhanced safety features, such as automatic shut-off and sealed combustion.

To convert a wood-burning fireplace to gas, you'll need to:

1. Assess your fireplace and chimney: Before converting to gas, you'll need to have your fireplace and chimney inspected by a professional to ensure they are structurally sound and compatible with gas burning. This may involve a visual inspection, as well as a thorough cleaning and any necessary repairs.

2. Choose your gas insert or log set: There are two main options for converting a wood-burning fireplace to gas: a gas insert or a gas log set. A gas insert is a self-contained unit that fits inside your existing fireplace and provides a sealed, efficient combustion system. A gas log set, on the other hand, is a collection of ceramic logs and burners that sit inside your fireplace and create a realistic flame effect.

3. Install a gas line and valve: To fuel your new gas fireplace, you'll need to have a gas line and valve installed by a licensed professional. This may involve running a new line from your home's main gas supply or connecting to an existing line, depending on your home's setup and local codes.

4. Modify your chimney and venting: Depending on the type of gas fireplace you choose, you may need to modify your chimney and venting system to ensure proper exhaust and air flow. This may involve installing a new chimney liner, cap, or damper, or sealing off the top of your chimney to prevent drafts and moisture intrusion.

5. Install and test your new gas fireplace: Once your gas line, venting, and fireplace components are in place, a professional installer will need to connect and test your new gas fireplace to ensure it is operating safely and efficiently. This may involve adjusting the gas pressure, calibrating the thermostat and remote control, and checking for any leaks or malfunctions.

By following these steps and working with a qualified professional, you can successfully convert your wood-burning fireplace to gas and enjoy the convenience, efficiency, and safety of a modern gas fireplace.

Converting from Gas to Wood-Burning:

While less common than converting from wood to gas, some homeowners may choose to convert their gas fireplace back to wood-burning for a more traditional and rustic experience. Converting from gas to wood-burning can be a more involved and costly process than the reverse, but it can be done with the right planning and professional help.

To convert a gas fireplace to wood-burning, you'll need to:

1. Assess your fireplace and chimney: Just like with a gas conversion, you'll need to have your fireplace and chimney inspected by a professional to ensure they are structurally sound and compatible with wood-burning. This may involve a visual inspection, as well as a thorough cleaning and any necessary repairs.

2. Remove your gas insert or log set: If you have a gas insert or log set installed in your fireplace, you'll need to have it safely removed and disposed of by a professional. This may involve disconnecting the gas line, removing the insert or log set, and sealing off any openings or vents.

3. Install a new wood-burning grate and liner: To burn wood safely and efficiently in your fireplace, you'll need to install a new metal grate to hold the logs and a new chimney liner to protect your chimney from heat and corrosion. The grate should be sized appropriately for your fireplace opening, and the liner should be made of stainless steel or another heat-resistant material.

4. Modify your chimney and venting: Depending on the condition and design of your chimney, you may need to make some modifications to ensure proper venting and air flow for wood-burning. This may involve installing a new chimney cap, damper, or flue, or repairing any cracks, gaps, or other damage to the chimney structure.

5. Test and enjoy your new wood-burning fireplace: Once your new grate, liner, and chimney components are in place, you can begin using your wood-burning fireplace. Be sure to follow all safety guidelines and best practices for building, tending, and extinguishing your fires, and have your chimney professionally inspected and cleaned at least once a year to ensure optimal performance and safety.

While converting from gas to wood-burning can be a more complex and expensive process than converting from wood to gas, it can be a worthwhile investment for homeowners who value the ambiance, warmth, and tradition of a real wood fire. By working with a qualified professional and carefully planning and executing your conversion, you can successfully transform your gas fireplace into a beautiful and functional wood-burning hearth.

Considerations for Both Types of Conversions:

Regardless of whether you're converting from wood to gas or vice versa, there are some key considerations to keep in mind to ensure a safe, successful, and satisfying conversion:

1. Local codes and permits: Before beginning any fireplace conversion, be sure to check with your local building department and fire marshal to ensure compliance with all relevant codes and regulations. You may need to obtain permits, inspections, or certifications for your conversion, depending on your location and the scope of the project.

2. Fuel availability and cost: Consider the availability and cost of your new fuel source, whether it's natural gas, propane, or firewood. Make sure you have reliable access to your fuel of choice, and factor in any ongoing costs or maintenance requirements.

3. Heating needs and efficiency: Think about your heating needs and preferences, as well as the size and layout of your home, when choosing a new fireplace type and fuel source. Gas fireplaces tend to be more efficient and controllable than wood-burning models, but wood fires can provide a more natural and radiant heat.

4. Aesthetics and design: Consider how your new fireplace will look and integrate with your home's existing decor and architecture. Choose materials, finishes, and accessories that complement your style and provide a cohesive, attractive look.

5. Professional installation and maintenance: Always work with a qualified and experienced professional for any fireplace conversion or installation project. Improper installation or maintenance can lead to safety hazards, performance issues, and costly repairs down the line.

By keeping these considerations in mind and working with a trusted professional, you can ensure a safe, successful, and satisfying fireplace conversion that will provide warmth, comfort, and enjoyment for years to come.

What to know before adding a new fireplace to your home

Adding a new fireplace to your home can be a great way to enhance your living space, increase your home's value, and create a cozy, inviting atmosphere. However, before embarking on this project, there are several important factors to consider to ensure a safe, successful, and satisfying installation. In this section, we'll explore what you need to know before adding a new fireplace to your home, including key considerations, steps, and best practices.

1. Determine Your Goals and Needs:

Before adding a new fireplace to your home, it's important to determine your goals and needs for the project. Some key questions to ask yourself include:

- What is the primary purpose of the fireplace? Is it for heating, ambiance, or both?
- What type of fuel do you want to use? Wood, gas, electric, or pellet?
- Where do you want to locate the fireplace? In a living room, bedroom, basement, or outdoor space?
- What style and design do you want for the fireplace? Traditional, modern, rustic, or something else?
- What is your budget for the project, including installation, materials, and ongoing fuel and maintenance costs?

By answering these questions and clarifying your goals and needs upfront, you can help guide your decision-making process and ensure a fireplace installation that meets your expectations and fits your lifestyle.

2. Assess Your Home's Structure and Layout:

Before adding a new fireplace, you'll need to assess your home's existing structure and layout to determine the feasibility and requirements of the installation. Some key factors to consider include:

- The location and size of the room where you want to install the fireplace.
- The proximity of the proposed fireplace location to combustible materials, such as walls, floors, and furniture.
- The availability and accessibility of fuel sources, such as gas lines, electrical outlets, or chimney flues.
- The structural integrity and load-bearing capacity of the floor and walls around the proposed fireplace location.
- The ventilation and air flow requirements for the type of fireplace you want to install.

To assess these factors and ensure a safe and code-compliant installation, it's important to work with a qualified professional, such as a fireplace installer, contractor, or architect. They can help you evaluate your home's structure and layout, identify any potential challenges or limitations, and recommend the best options for your specific needs and goals.

3. Choose Your Fireplace Type and Fuel Source:

Once you've determined your goals and assessed your home's structure, the next step is to choose the type of fireplace and fuel source that best fits your needs and preferences. Some common options include:

- Wood-burning fireplaces: These traditional fireplaces burn wood logs to create heat and ambiance. They require a chimney for venting and can be more labor-intensive to maintain than other types of fireplaces.

- Gas fireplaces: These fireplaces use natural gas or propane to create a realistic flame and heat output. They can be vented through a chimney or directly through an exterior wall, and offer convenient features like remote control and thermostat operation.

- Electric fireplaces: These fireplaces use electricity to create a simulated flame and heat output. They don't require venting and can be installed virtually anywhere in your home, making them a popular choice for apartments, condos, and smaller spaces.

- Pellet fireplaces: These fireplaces burn compressed wood or biomass pellets to create heat and a small amount of flame. They require a vent for exhaust and can be more efficient and environmentally friendly than traditional wood-burning fireplaces.

When choosing your fireplace type and fuel source, consider factors like your heating needs, fuel availability and cost, maintenance requirements, and aesthetic preferences. Work with a qualified professional to help you select the best option for your home and ensure a safe and efficient installation.

4. Plan for Proper Venting and Chimney Installation:
Proper venting and chimney installation are critical for the safe and efficient operation of any fireplace. Depending on the type of fireplace you choose, you may need to install a new chimney, modify an existing one, or use a direct vent or ventless system. Some key considerations for venting and chimney installation include:

- The height, size, and location of the chimney in relation to your home's roof and surrounding structures.

- The type and quality of the chimney liner, which protects the chimney from heat and corrosion and ensures proper exhaust flow.
- The installation of a chimney cap and spark arrestor to prevent moisture, debris, and pests from entering the chimney and to contain any stray sparks or embers.
- The clearance and distance requirements between the chimney and any combustible materials, such as roof shingles, siding, or tree branches.

To ensure a safe and code-compliant venting and chimney installation, it's important to work with a certified chimney professional or fireplace installer. They can assess your home's specific needs and requirements, recommend the best venting options, and ensure that all components are installed and maintained properly.

5. Consider the Costs and Returns:

Adding a new fireplace to your home can be a significant investment, with costs ranging from a few thousand to tens of thousands of dollars depending on the type, size, and complexity of the installation. Before embarking on this project, it's important to carefully consider the costs and potential returns of the investment. Some key factors to consider include:

- The upfront costs of the fireplace unit, installation, and any necessary structural or ventilation modifications.
- The ongoing costs of fuel, maintenance, and repairs over the life of the fireplace.
- The potential energy savings or costs associated with using the fireplace as a supplemental or primary heat source.
- The potential impact on your home's resale value and marketability, as fireplaces are often seen as a desirable amenity by homebuyers.

- The intangible benefits of the fireplace, such as increased comfort, ambiance, and enjoyment of your living space.

To help manage the costs and maximize the returns of your fireplace installation, consider working with a qualified professional to develop a detailed project plan and budget. Look for opportunities to save money on materials and labor, such as by choosing a pre-fabricated or modular fireplace unit or by doing some of the preparation work yourself. And be sure to factor in the long-term costs and benefits of the fireplace when making your decision, rather than just focusing on the upfront expenses.

6. Obtain Necessary Permits and Inspections:
Before beginning any fireplace installation project, it's important to obtain all necessary permits and inspections from your local building department and fire authority. Depending on your location and the scope of the project, you may need to submit plans, pay fees, and schedule inspections at various stages of the installation process. Some common permits and inspections required for fireplace installations include:

- Building permits for any structural modifications or additions to your home.
- Electrical permits for any new or modified electrical wiring or components.
- Gas permits for any new or modified gas lines or connections.
- Ventilation and chimney permits for any new or modified venting systems or chimneys.
- Final inspections to ensure that the fireplace and all related components are installed safely and in compliance with all applicable codes and standards.

Failing to obtain necessary permits and inspections can result in costly fines, legal liabilities, and even the need to remove or modify the fireplace installation. To avoid these risks and ensure a safe and compliant installation, work with a qualified professional who is familiar with local building codes and permitting requirements, and be sure to schedule all required inspections and approvals before using your new fireplace.

7. Plan for Proper Use and Maintenance:

Finally, before adding a new fireplace to your home, it's important to plan for the proper use and maintenance of the unit to ensure its safety, efficiency, and longevity. Some key considerations for use and maintenance include:

- Following all manufacturer's instructions and recommendations for the safe and proper operation of the fireplace, including any startup, shutdown, and emergency procedures.
- Using only approved and properly seasoned fuel sources, such as dry, hardwood logs for wood-burning fireplaces or the specified type and grade of gas for gas fireplaces.
- Regularly cleaning and inspecting the fireplace and related components, such as the chimney, flue, and gas or electrical connections, to ensure proper function and prevent potential hazards.
- Scheduling annual professional maintenance and inspections to identify and address any potential issues or concerns before they become more serious or costly to repair.
- Installing and maintaining proper safety features, such as smoke and carbon monoxide detectors, fire extinguishers, and chimney caps or screens, to protect against potential fire or health hazards.

By planning for the proper use and maintenance of your new fireplace, you can help ensure its safe and efficient operation, prolong its lifespan, and maximize its benefits and enjoyment for your home and family.

In Conclusion:

Adding a new fireplace to your home can be a rewarding and transformative project, but it's important to approach it with careful planning, research, and professional guidance. By determining your goals and needs, assessing your home's structure and layout, choosing the right fireplace type and fuel source, planning for proper venting and chimney installation, considering the costs and returns, obtaining necessary permits and inspections, and planning for proper use and maintenance, you can help ensure a safe, successful, and satisfying fireplace installation that will provide warmth, comfort, and enjoyment for years to come.

Conclusion

Throughout this comprehensive guide, we've explored the many facets of caring for and enjoying fireplaces in your home. From the basics of how fireplaces and chimneys work to the intricacies of maintaining and troubleshooting different types of fireplaces, we've covered a wide range of topics to help you become a true fireplace aficionado.

We've delved into the joys and challenges of wood-burning fireplaces, offering practical tips and techniques for choosing, storing, and burning the best firewood, as well as keeping your wood-burning fireplace and chimney in top shape. We've also explored the convenience and efficiency of gas fireplaces, with guidance on safe operation, cleaning, and maintenance, as well as identifying and fixing common issues.

In addition to the practical aspects of fireplace care, we've also considered the aesthetic and functional benefits of fireplaces, with ideas for upgrading and enhancing the beauty and performance of your hearth. Whether you're looking to convert an old fireplace to a new fuel source, add a fireplace to a new room or outdoor space, or simply refresh the look of your existing fireplace, we've provided inspiration and guidance to help you achieve your goals.

Most importantly, we've emphasized the critical importance of fireplace and chimney safety throughout this book. From essential fire safety practices and chimney maintenance tips to advice on childproofing and preventing accidents, we've provided a wealth of information to help you enjoy your fireplace with peace of mind and confidence.

In the end, the key to being a successful fireplace owner is a combination of knowledge, diligence, and proactive care. By understanding the fundamentals of how your fireplace works, staying on top of regular cleaning and maintenance tasks, and knowing when to call in the pros for expert help, you can ensure that your fireplace remains a safe, efficient, and enjoyable centerpiece of your home for years to come.

So whether you're curling up by a crackling wood fire on a chilly winter's eve, basking in the glow of a sleek gas insert, or enjoying the warmth and ambiance of a fireplace in any season, we hope that this guide has equipped you with the tools and knowledge you need to make the most of this timeless and beloved feature of the home.

As you embark on your journey as a fireplace aficionado, remember to always prioritize safety, stay curious and proactive in your learning and care, and take the time to savor the simple, immeasurable pleasures of a well-tended hearth. Here's to many cozy, memorable, and meaningful moments by the fire!